knit a
MONSTER NURSERY

Practical and Playful Knitted Baby Patterns

Rebecca Danger

Martingale®
Create with Confidence

To Presley, my little monster

Mission Statement

Dedicated to providing quality products
and service to inspire creativity.

CREDITS

President & CEO * Tom Wierzbicki
Editor in Chief * Mary V. Green
Design Director * Paula Schlosser
Managing Editor * Karen Costello Soltys
Technical Editor * Ursula Reikes
Copy Editor * Marcy Heffernan
Production Manager * Regina Girard
Cover & Text Designer * Adrienne Smitke
Illustrators * Sue Mattero & Adrienne Smitke
Photographer * Brent Kane

Knit a Monster Nursery:
Practical and Playful Knitted Baby Patterns
© 2012 by Rebecca Danger

Create with Confidence

Martingale®
19021 120th Ave. NE, Suite 102
Bothell, WA 98011 USA
ShopMartingale.com

Printed in China
17 16 15 14 13 12   8 7 6 5 4 3 2 1

Library of Congress Cataloging-in-Publication Data is
available upon request.

ISBN: 978-1-60468-149-9

Contents

Introduction / 5

Monster-Knitting Guidelines and Techniques / 6

Monster-Making University / 15

Knitting for Little Monsters / 20

Making Your Own Monster Nursery / 21

Monster Pocket Sweater / 26

Monster Booties / 30

Monster-Face Hat / 33

Pointy Monster Hat / 36

Snuggly Monster Blankie Friend / 40

Cuddly Monster Blankie / 44

Pocket Blankie with Monster Friend / 48

Monster Mobile / 54

Monster Swings 64

Monster Bookends / 77

Monster Pillows / 82

Monster Tissue and Wipes Box Covers / 86

Monster Chair / 90

Stack O' Monsters / 93

Monster Blocks / 100

Monster Rattles / 104

Abbreviations/Glossary / 108

Where to Get the Goods / 110

Standard Yarn-Weight System / 111

Acknowledgments / 112

Introduction

Hello and welcome to *Knit a Monster Nursery*! In the following pages, you'll find lots of projects to welcome new little monsters into your life. In fact, these pages contain an entire room's worth of knits. Just check out the pictures on page 22 to see the projects in action in my own monster nursery!

Not just for babies, the projects in this book are great for kids and adults alike. Though I used all the projects to decorate my son Presley's room, there is nothing to say that any of these projects couldn't be used outside of a nursery as well.

Presley was my true inspiration for every project in this book. I started writing this book right after he was born, and absolutely the best part of working on it was being able to see his reaction to everything I was creating. The mobile was probably the biggest hit; when he was tiny, he would lie in his crib and coo at it for an hour every day before he was ready to get up. Each and every monster I showed him, he would reach out and grab for. Sometimes they would even make him laugh out loud or "squee" with delight. You'll also notice many, many striped projects, since every time I'd show him something with stripes he'd be just mesmerized. I'm pleased to be able to offer you these mom and baby tested-and-approved projects.

A big part of this book was the desire I had to let my kiddo know how much I loved him from day one. For me that meant creating a wonderfully distinctive space and truly unique items just for him. I hope that you're able to connect to the babies (and others) in your life and show them how much you love them in the same way through these projects.

I wish you many hours of monster-filled knitting!

Rebecca Danger

Monster-Knitting Guidelines and Techniques

I love clever knitting techniques. There is nothing better for me than a really innovative way of doing something complicated. Though I assume you have a basic knitting knowledge, I have used a few tricky techniques in this book that you may not be familiar with. So as not to completely confuse you, I've included more detailed descriptions of them below.

MONSTER GAUGES

Though many of the projects in this book call for a specific gauge, my monster patterns do not. You can pick which size yarn and needles to use. Simply use smaller needles than those recommended for your yarn to create a tighter knit fabric so that the stuffing doesn't show through. My rule of thumb is to go down two or three needle sizes from the smallest recommended needle size for your yarn. For example, Cascade 220 Superwash is recommended to be knit on a U.S. size 6 (4.25 mm) or 7 (4.5 mm) needle; I used a U.S. size 4 (3.5 mm) needle. Depending on your personal knitting style, this may be right on for you, or you may want to go up or down a size.

In "Monster Mobile" on page 54, the patterns all recommend using sock yarn to make a small monster. Because sock yarn already calls for a small needle, I recommend using a U.S. size 1 (2.25 mm) or 0 (2 mm) depending on how loose your gauge is. Although you could use a U.S. size 00 (1.75 mm), you really don't need to go that tiny. You can also use heavier-weight yarn and bigger needles to knit the mini monsters; they just won't be as mini.

Because you can pick your yarn weight and needle size, you can make all sorts of sizes of monsters from each one of my patterns. I've included a couple of samples of some projects to give you a general idea of what size monster you'll get with different yarn and needle sizes. Just remember: heavier-weight yarn and bigger needles mean bigger monsters, while lighter-weight yarn and smaller needles mean smaller monsters.

MONSTER YARDAGE

For just the monster patterns, determining the yardage needed can be a little tricky. Since you're picking the yarn and needles you use, it's hard for me to be exact with the amount of yarn to use. Obviously, a project knit with sock yarn and U.S. size 1 (2.25 mm) needles will take way less yardage than a project knit with chunky yarn and U.S. size 11 (8 mm) needles. On the bigger needles, there's simply more needle to go around, therefore more yarn is needed.

The recommended yardage for the larger monster patterns in this book is for the U.S. size 4 (3.5 mm) to 9 (5.5 mm) needle range. Yes, you can *probably* sneak a monster through on your 10s, but I would add an extra 20 to 40 yards of yarn just to be safe. I would add even more—up to, say, 100 yards over the recommended amount—if you're using anything larger. Just remember, smaller needles mean you'll need the low end of the recommended yardage, and bigger needles mean you'll need the higher end of recommended yardage. Got it? Since I very notoriously run out of yarn with just an ear to go, my rule is to just buy more than I think I'll need. I mean, is there really such a thing as *too much* yarn? My answer is, "No."

MAGIC LOOP METHOD

Let's face it, I love the Magic Loop method. Most every pattern in this book that is knit in the round uses this method. The Magic Loop method is the best. It's quick, easy, you can use one length needle for everything, there's no danger of stitches slipping from your double-pointed needles, you don't have to transfer to double-pointed needles as you decrease, your project transports easily, it's easier to knit with the Magic Loop than double-pointed needles when you have a baby on your lap, it's more fun (seriously)—I could go on and on. However, many people find the Magic Loop to be, well, rather terrifying, and I respect that. Though I encourage you to take the plunge and learn the Magic Loop method, it's really just one way of knitting in the round. You like double-pointed needles? Those work too. You like knitting in the round on two circular needles? Have at it. All of my patterns that call for the Magic Loop method can easily be knit using any other way of knitting in the round as well: on a set of double-pointed needles, two circular needles, or a short circular needle instead (for circular needles, you'll have to be the judge of length depending on how big or small your project is).

Let's break down the Magic Loop method and make it easy. Grab a circular knitting needle with a 40" or longer cable—the more flexible the cable, the better. You will need this extra long cable to make the "loop" for the Magic Loop method. Cast on your stitches as you would normally (fig. 1).

Now, slide the stitches to the center of the cable and find the center point of the stitches so you can divide them in half. Pull the cable out at this point (fig. 2).

Slide the stitches back up onto the needles, with half the stitches on the front needle and half the stitches on the back needle. The working yarn should be coming from the stitches on the back needle (fig. 3).

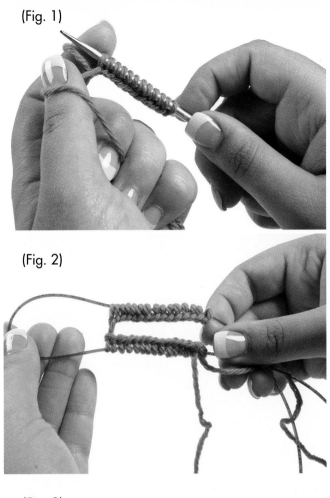

(Fig. 1)

(Fig. 2)

(Fig. 3)

monster-knitting guidelines and techniques

(Fig. 4)

With the cast-on edge facing inward to avoid twisted stitches, get ready to knit in the round. First, pull the back needle out so that about half the cable is sticking out to the left-hand side and the other half of the cable is sticking out to the right-hand side (fig. 4).

Now, with the working yarn over and behind the cable of the back needle, knit across the stitches on the front needle (fig. 5). (I generally place a marker about two to four stitches in so I know this is the beginning of my round.) Once you get to the end of that needle, pull the needles so that all the stitches are back on the needles.

Turn your work around, pull the back needle out again as you did to start, and with the working yarn over and behind the cable of the back needle, knit across the second needle of stitches (fig. 6).

Eureka! You're Magic Looping! Now do this 1,000 times until you're really comfortable with it.

(Fig. 5)

Little Magic Loop

I have found that for the mobile monsters (page 54) and other small Magic Loop projects, you can get away with using a 32" circular needle. This length works best for small projects knit on a U.S. size 2 (2.75 mm) needle or smaller. In fact, it's sometimes *easier* for these smaller projects to have a slightly shorter cable.

(Fig. 6)

PROVISIONAL CAST ON USING WASTE YARN

The provisional cast on is one of those nifty knitting techniques that I love. I remember the first time I used it and got it figured out, it was one of those total "Aha!" moments. I love those kinds of moments.

A provisional cast on is a cast on that leaves "live" stitches for you to come back to later. Clever, huh? Though there are a couple ways to do a provisional cast on, I really prefer the one using waste yarn. I am so crochet-inept that the method where you start with a crochet chain just baffles me. If you like the crochet-chain version, you can use it in place of the waste-yarn method I explain here.

Grab your needles, the end of your working yarn, and a piece of waste yarn several times longer than your finished cast on will be.

Make a slipknot in your working yarn and place it on your needles (fig. 7). You only need to leave a short tail, just long enough to weave in when you're done. You'll only be working with the yarn coming from your skein.

Hold the waste yarn in front of your working yarn and your slipknot in your right hand (fig. 8).

Move your working yarn under the waste yarn (fig. 9), then in front of the waste yarn and up and over the top of the needle (fig. 10).

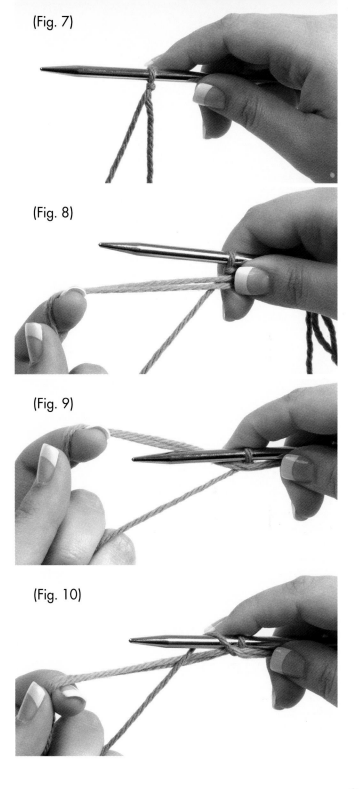

(Fig. 7)

(Fig. 8)

(Fig. 9)

(Fig. 10)

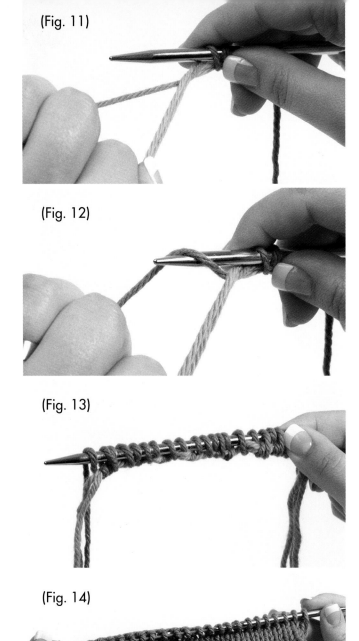

(Fig. 11)

(Fig. 12)

(Fig. 13)

(Fig. 14)

Now, move your working yarn under and to the back of the waste yarn (fig. 11), then over the top of the needle from front to back (fig. 12).

Repeat these two steps, until you have the number of stitches required for your project, counting *only the number of stitches on your needle* (fig. 13). Wrap the waste yarn around the working yarn and turn the work.

With this cast on, every other stitch will be twisted on the waste yarn, so when you come to those stitches, knit into the back of those stitches on your first round. That will ensure the stitches are no longer twisted.

Work as instructed for your project. This is what your work will look like once you've knit a few rows. See the live loops (fig. 14)?

When you're ready to work the stitches on the waste yarn, you'll simply slip them to your needle and remove the waste yarn.

Ta-da! Nifty, huh?

A Personal Quirk

When I do the provisional cast on with the waste yarn, I fold my piece of waste yarn in half to make it thicker. Although I was never instructed to do it this way, it seems to work pretty well for making a slightly thicker place to hold those live stitches—so you might like to give it a try, too!

MAKING STUFFED RINGS

As I began creating the projects in this book, I realized many, many baby projects involve rings. I've used a fairly simple, seamless way of knitting these shapes, but it is a little tricky. Below you will find a step-by-step explanation of how to make them.

Using the provisional cast on with waste yarn (page 9), use your working yarn to cast on the required number of stitches on a circular needle long enough for the Magic Loop method (fig. 15).

Now, turn your work and knit across the stitches you just cast on (fig. 16).

When you get to the end of the row, slide your stitches to the middle of the cable and divide half of the stitches to each needle tip to set up working in the round using the Magic Loop method (fig. 17).

Working from the last stitch you knit to the first stitch on the other needle tip, join to begin working in the round. Be doubly sure not to twist your stitches on this step (fig. 18).

Once you reach the end of the project and you're ready to bind off, slip the provisional cast-on stitches to a second circular needle (of any length) and remove the waste yarn (fig. 19).

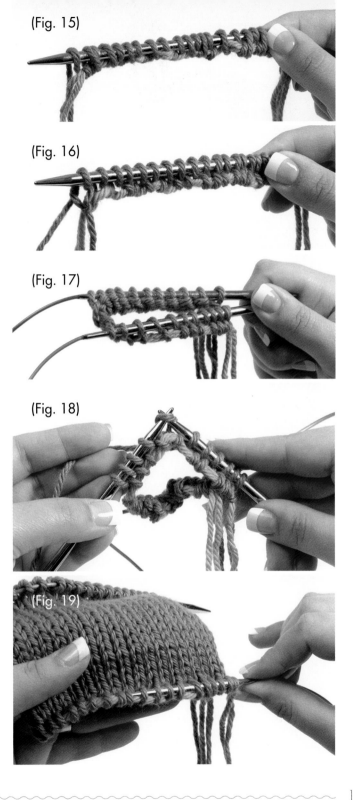

(Fig. 15)

(Fig. 16)

(Fig. 17)

(Fig. 18)

(Fig. 19)

(Fig. 20)

(Fig. 21)

(Fig. 22)

(Fig. 23)

Move that new needle up through the center of your project so that it's right next to the needle you've been working on (fig. 20).

This will fold your piece and place the first and the last rounds next to each other, essentially "halfing" the length of your piece (fig. 21).

Now, cut your yarn, leaving an extra-long tail (about four times the circumference of your project). Grab a tapestry needle and begin to work the Kitchener stitch, moving from the beginning of the round you just completed, to the provisional cast-on stitches (fig. 22).

Remember, the provisional cast on will leave every other stitch twisted, so untwist them as you come to them. Continue using the Kitchener stitch around the ring, stopping every couple of inches to stuff the ring. If you end up a stitch short at the end, just pick one up (fig. 23).

Weave in your ends and twist the Kitchener seam to the inside of the ring. Voilà—a knitted doughnut.

How About Those Double-Pointed Needles?

I've written these directions for making rings using the Magic Loop method because I think it's the easiest way to do it. If you want to use double-pointed needles instead, cast all of your stitches onto one needle, knit the row across that needle, as above, and split the stitches off onto three double-pointed needles as you knit the first round. I still recommend switching to a circular needle to Kitchener stitch the ring shut though, since it will more securely hold the stitches as you come to them and there will be no worry of slipped stitches.

monster-knitting guidelines and techniques

IN THE (BACKWARD) LOOP

Look, Ma! I'm casting on backward! One of my favorite monster techniques for adding stitches mid-round or mid-row is the backward-loop cast on. Though it may sound impossible, it's super easy to do. Just grab your working yarn, make a loop around your thumb or index finger (from back to front), and slip it onto your needle (fig. 24). You just added a stitch! Repeat for as many stitches as called for (fig. 25). It's as easy as taking candy from a baby. (Babies really shouldn't have candy anyway!)

EXTRA HELP

Does a term or knitting technique still have you confused, even after my spectacular guidelines? No worries, even we knitting superheroes sometimes need to ask for help! Just remember, the Internet is your friend. The best places to go for help are knittinghelp.com, youtube.com, and your local yarn shop. Knittinghelp.com offers fantastic videos to help you every step of the way. If you just search for the confusing term on YouTube, there are generally a plethora of videos to help. Or, if you buy your supplies at a local yarn shop, the staff will be more than happy to help you out with any knitting questions you might have. They're not as good on the "What's the meaning of life?"-type questions, though. Trust me, I've asked. But you could ask them if there is a particular knitting reference book they recommend.

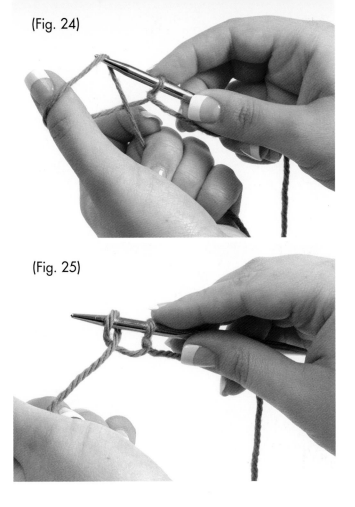

(Fig. 24)

(Fig. 25)

Monster-Making University

Knitting monsters is lots of fun, but they definitely aren't your run-of-the-mill sweater projects! I use a few basic tricks and tips you should be aware of before you start. Read through the general guidelines below; then get knitting!

LEGS TO BODY

Probably the trickiest part of my monster patterns is moving from the legs to the body on the monsters where the body/legs/head are all knit as one unit.

Don't worry, it's as easy as 1-2-3! When you've finished the first leg, including the backward-loop cast-on stitches, cut your yarn and transfer these stitches to your circular needle by sliding half the leg stitches onto the front needle and half the leg stitches on the back needle, with the cast-on stitches toward the right end of the back needle (fig. 26).

Make a second leg and cut your yarn, leaving a 10" tail for sewing the body closed at the end. Divide the second leg's stitches on your stitch holder, with half the leg stitches on one side and half the leg stitches plus the cast-on stitches on the other side. Now, transfer these stitches onto the circular needle, just as they're divided on your stitch holder, putting half the leg stitches plus the cast-on stitches on the *front* needle and half the leg stitches on the *back* needle. There will be a few cast-on stitches on each needle between the first and second leg. You now have a new beginning of the round in the middle of your monster's second leg (fig. 27).

Now that you've transferred the individual leg stitches to your circular needle, you'll join your working yarn as you begin the body. This will set you up to easily make

(Fig. 26)

(Fig. 27)

body-shaping decreases directly on the sides of the monster without too much tricky counting, especially if you use the Magic Loop method to knit the body. Easy peasy, lemon squeezy!

UP, DOWN, TURN AROUND

Many of the patterns call for you to turn something inside out and use the three-needle bind off on your live stitches, since it makes a nice finished seam. If you're not using the Magic Loop method (seriously, here's another benefit, just go learn it!), you'll probably want to transfer your stitches to a circular needle of any size to turn your item inside out. It's much, much easier and much, much less terrifying to thread the needle points of your circular needle through the bottom opening to easily turn something inside out than it is using any other method.

When you do turn your item inside out, you might notice that as you use the three-needle bind off, your yarn will be coming from the first stitch in the front, instead of the last stitch in the back like normal. No biggie! This is what it's supposed to look like, so just power on through.

WEAVING IN THE ENDS

While beautiful finishing is important for some of the projects in this book (specifically the monster projects), there is a little more wiggle room. I'll let you in on a little secret: Even though I use the obligatory "weave in the ends" in all of the monster patterns, I don't ever weave in the ends. Monsters are going to have a lovely inside filled with fluff that will hide the ends, so the most I usually do is to just pull the ends to the inside of the project, and voilà! I'm done. All ends are hidden on the inside. I also generally leave a long tail when I cast on so that I can use that tail to sew the body parts to the torso in the end, leaving me with even less ends to worry about. Once a limb is sewn to the torso, I pull the yarn through the body right where I'm sewing the limb on, pull it out the opposite side of the body, and cut the yarn flush to the body. Instantly hides that tail every time!

I'M STUFFED

I really like to think of stuffing as sculpting, more than just finishing. Stuffing your monster is what can make or break the final project. How your monster comes out in the end is really based on how much time and effort you put into the stuffing. You may notice on some of my samples that the same monster pattern knit with different sizes of yarn and needles, can create monsters that are the same size.

Good stuffing technique comes completely from practice. I've stuffed a lot of monsters, and I swear that I learn something from each and every one I stuff.

When it comes to stuffing a monster, make sure to give yourself lots of time. Look at your monster from all sides: got a lump, valley, or hunchback? Smoosh the stuffing around to shape it, or add a little more until it looks right. There is a lot of squashing and rolling and adding bits of fluff here and there when I work. If you keep stuffing and stuffing and it's just not looking right, it might be time to take all the stuffing out and start again. Make sure to use my samples; that's what they're there for!

I'm asked all the time what type of stuffing I use. Honestly, I use the cheapest stuffing I can find. When I find it on sale I buy 10 bags of the stuff—which always means strange looks from the craft-store clerk. Especially when they ask what it's for, and I tell them I knit monsters. But then again, I get the same reaction in yarn shops, so I'm pretty used to it. Anyway, I go through bags of this stuff, and I can't really tell a difference between the brands. I just like to make sure I buy a hypoallergenic type, especially when my projects are intended for babies. Organic stuffing would also be a good choice for babies.

SEW WHAT?

I love making up my monsters, because that's when the personality starts to show through. I start by stuffing all the different limbs, and then setting the main monster body in my lap. I play around with how the monster will look by testing arm, ear, and leg placement with straight pins before I get to stitching anything down. (I say straight pins, but I honestly use extra tapestry needles to pin on the limbs. I keep a major stash of them because they just seem to work for me.) Pinning all the limbs first let's me match everything up and sew everything on at the same height.

So I pin, then move, then pin, then move. Then I move the
stuffing around a bit, and then pin some more. When I'm
really happy with how everything looks, I begin to sew.

The easiest way to sew on the arms, legs, or feet is
to flatten the open, cast-on edge of the appendage and
attach that edge to the body. This will make your limbs
hang down to the sides, giving your critter a natural look.
(Or, at least as natural as a stuffed, knitted monster can
look.) For the actual attaching, I find using a whipstitch—
essentially up, over, and around the top of the limb—
works the best. I use the same whipstitch to attach ears,
or if a monster has feet attached to the outside of its body
(fig. 28).

When the monster has a flat seam, like Vinny V, the
Small-Ears Monster (page 69), I stitch it up with a running
stitch instead. I like to attach legs to the inside of the seam
before I start to shut the bottom seam so I can hide the leg
attachment (fig. 29).

Once the legs are attached, I zip across the bottom
seam with a running stitch to close the body (fig. 30).

Those are pretty much the only two types of seams
I use when assembling monsters. I do have a new foot
in this book that is knit very similarly to a bootie. For the
bottom seam I use a stitch-to-stitch mattress stitch (page
32) to disguise the seam as much as possible. For seam-
ing the back of the chair and the hat, I use a row-to-row
mattress stitch (page 35).

For the best results, just pin, pin, pin; play around a
lot with stuffing; study the samples in the photos; and do
what feels right. Making monsters is about having fun—
play around to find what works best for you. And make
lots and lots of monsters, since practice makes perfect!

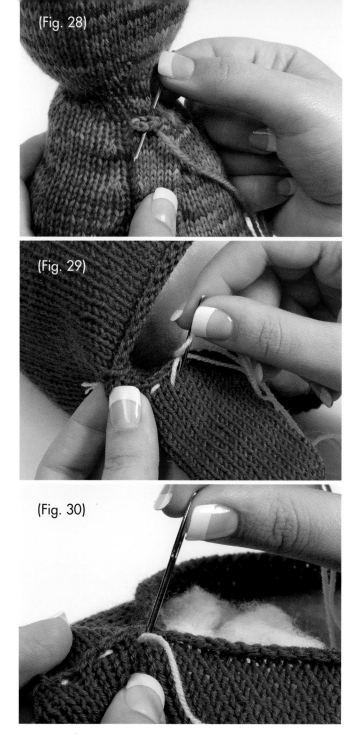

(Fig. 28)

(Fig. 29)

(Fig. 30)

BELLY BUTTONS

Innies, outies, we've all got a belly button, right? Then monsters should have them too! Using a single strand of yarn and a tapestry needle, and referring to the photos for placement, make an X in the middle of your monster's belly as you're stuffing the body. Before you close up your monster, pull the ends to the inside and tie them in a small knot to make sure the belly button stays in place.

HERE'S LOOKING AT YOU

Oh, the face! This is where your monster's individual personality will come shining through. I think this is the toughest part and probably where I spend the majority of my monster-making time. Yes, it can be challenging, but don't fret and lose sleep over your monster faces. I just talk to my half-finished monster to decide what is going to look right on him or her and keep moving and remaking the facial features until I'm really happy with what I see. When making toys for babies and kids under age three, safety must be your first concern. I love how my normal felt teeth and safety eyes look, but for this book I've added a lot of other faces as well. Safety eyes and felt

mouths can be fairly easily removed by curious little fingers, so I've done a bit of experimenting with embroidery in this book. Check out the monster close-ups above for inspiration.

When embroidering faces, use your tapestry needle, some black yarn or embroidery floss, and your imagination. I use a running stitch or a backstitch, depending on how tricky I want to be, and act like I'm "drawing" on the face to make the facial features. Check out the pictures throughout this book for ideas, or grab a piece of paper and sketch what you'd like your monster's face to look like. The really great thing about embroidering on knitted fabric is that the stitches and rows can act as a grid, sort of like a cross-stitch cloth, so you can be as "even" (or not) as you want to be. I just kind of wing it most of the time. Remember that you can always cut off your attempt and try again!

When working faces with safety eyes and felt teeth, move the pieces around until they look just right before attaching anything. Eyes look weird? Try the next size up or down. Mouth just not feeling "right?" Cut a new one. Seriously, it can change the whole feel of the monster.

For the spikey, toothy-mouthed monsters, grab your scissors and some white felt. Using your monster's face as a gauge for width, cut a rectangle of white felt, making sure to cut one long edge super straight. Then, using extra-sharp scissors, cut up and down at an angle on the not-as-straight edge to create little pointy teeth. Be careful not to cut too far down between the teeth or the felt will want to pull apart as you're gluing it onto the face. Be careful not to cut too shallow here either, or the teeth will look super bulky. There's nothing that says you have to be perfect, and you can recut the mouth as many times as you need to.

All aspects of monster making should be fun, and that goes for the face too. And remember, if your monster looks really odd, it will just give him more character!

I'VE GOT EYES IN THE BACK OF MY HEAD

If you do decide to use safety eyes on your monsters, I've included what size safety eyes I used for the samples I added eyes to. Now, as much as I would like to rule the world, this is only so you have a *general idea* what is going to look best. Because every knitter knits very differently, I recommend you have a range of safety eyes in your knitting tool kit so that, depending on how you've knit and stuffed your monster, you have options for eyes. I always try at least two sizes of eyes on each monster before deciding which I like best, and I suggest you do the same. You can purchase safety eyes at most craft stores, or on my website, www.dangercrafts.com. So you know what to buy, I use a general range of safety eyes from 6 mm to 18 mm.

Congratulations, you have graduated from Monster-Making University. I now deem you officially prepared to become a monster-knitting expert!

Want More?

I felt it would be better to fill the pages of this book with projects rather than directions. However, I know that finishing is probably what just about every knitter dreads and fears the most, so I have lots of awesome, in-depth finishing help (with lots and lots of pictures) on my blog: www.rebeccadanger.typepad.com.

Knitting for Little Monsters

Kids can be so much fun to knit for, but there are a few things you should take into consideration as you pull out your needles for any child-destined project.

PICKING KID-FRIENDLY YARNS

I thought very hard while picking yarns for this book to make sure I chose ones that are kid friendly. The most important things I look for when picking yarns for baby projects are super softness, machine washability, and bright color.

Babies are so sensitive, and if a project is going to touch baby skin, it's very important to pick something extra soft and, to me, preferably made of a natural fiber. I like merino and cotton, though it seems like I can find more and more super-soft acrylic yarns these days as well.

Besides being soft, I want my baby yarns to machine-wash well. When my baby was born, several folks gave me hand-knit sweaters that I had to hand wash. They were amazingly gorgeous, of course, but being a busy new mom who was writing a book, I ended up rarely using any of those hand-wash sweaters. I was already doing so much laundry (how do such small people create so much laundry?) that I didn't have time to hand wash anything, not to mention the fact that I was terrified that those hand-wash-only sweaters would somehow make it into the normal laundry basket and get felted.

I think organic fibers are a great option for babies too, especially for a toy that is going to be in their mouth constantly. No, seriously, *constantly*. It is sort of unbelievable.

BUILT MONSTER TOUGH

Take extra care when assembling your knitted monster. Kids are tough on toys, and if you don't want your monsters to end up at the monster hospital for limb reattachment, you'll want to make your seams extra tough. Doubling up seams is not a bad idea; go back over your stitches twice. Tying knots and hiding them in the knit fabric is also a good precaution.

MONSTER SAFETY

Keep in mind that children under three should not be given toys with things like safety eyes, buttons, or ribbons that could possibly come off and be ingested or prove otherwise harmful. While I've used plastic safety eyes and buttons on several of the projects in this book, please use caution when using them on toys for babies and toddlers under three. Buttons are also considered unsafe for children under three, so if you use them, check regularly to be sure they're securely attached and that little fingers can't tear them off. Same goes for safety eyes; babies should not be left alone with a monster with safety yes, since the eyes can be pulled out from the knit fabric and choked on. As a new mom, I felt like everyone was constantly warning me about potential dangers, but I played everything by ear. I agree that buttons and safety eyes could be harmful, and I do recommend embroidering on faces for monsters for babies. That being said, I did let my kiddo play with lots of toys with safety eyes (since we have a few in my house), but I always watched him closely while he played with them. No matter what you decide as far as buttons and safety eyes, please just be aware and use your best judgment for you, your family, and under three-year old recipients of hand knits.

Making Your Own Monster Nursery

One of the best parts of writing this book is that I get to share my own monster nursery with you! One of my main goals is to inspire you to create your own special space for your little monster. In this section I've included some design ideas and sources to help you get started.

DESIGN BASICS

Though I currently focus on knit design, I have a design background and am way into all kinds of design. When I was pregnant, one of the biggest things on my mind was designing the nursery for my new kiddo. To start, I picked a color scheme from a piece of fabric that I loved. I feel like you can tie anything together in a room if you stick with a color scheme.

Since I knew I would be adding lots of punches of color with my monsters and other decorative items, I decided to go with the gray from the background of the fabric for my wall color. Picking gray in the Pacific Northwest seemed like a risky idea, since it's always gray outside here, but it has worked out as a great subtle canvas.

From there I decided to go with a really clean, modern feel for the furniture. I looked and looked and looked (and looked) at furniture everywhere, for months. Seriously, I didn't even order a single piece of my furniture until about three weeks before I was due! To decide what I wanted, I printed out pictures of the pieces I was thinking about and put them together on a piece of paper to see what I thought would look best together.

I stuck with pretty much all-white furniture since I wanted the focus to be on the decorations and monsters in the room. More than just focusing on the aesthetic, I

thought about the function of each piece of furniture for my kiddo Presley, from birth on up. I picked nine-cube shelves, in which I could store diapers and clothes and whatnot when he was a baby, and that he could use to display toys and books as he got bigger. Instead of a changing table, I chose a dresser with a changing pad on top, so he could use it in the future for clothes. I even picked a crib that changes to a toddler bed so we could get more use out of it.

I picked a comfy armchair for the room, rather than a rocking chair. I chose a houndstooth print, bold and fun, but still in my color scheme.

Presley and the monsters at home in the finished nursery

Once all the furniture was picked out, I was able to start adding necessities (like laundry baskets and changing-table-supply storage) and accessories (like wall art). The way I picked everything else for the room was to make sure it fit into my color scheme (and monster theme).

The gray nursery walls make a great backdrop for wall art.

Download these free monster embroidery patterns from my blog!

Instead of a rocking chair, I chose this comfy houndstooth-print chair.

These fabrics inspired the color scheme in Presley's nursery.

making your own monster nursery

CUSTOMIZE IT!

I think customizing is what makes design the most fun and really makes your room stand out from the crowd. At first, after deciding on a monster theme, I was disappointed to find there was not much monster-themed stuff out there. Instead of buying premade items, I ended up making most of the items in the room. I even switched out the legs on the dresser to make it a better height for a changing table! However, by the end of writing this book, I was finding more and more commercially made monster-themed nursery items—so keep your eyes peeled.

The Internet and blogosphere are full of ideas and directions to make everything. I'm not kidding, *everything*. In the end, I figured making things for the room was probably quicker (and cheaper) than shopping for them! And, it was really special for my kiddo and way more fun for me.

PAINTINGS

Harkening back to my college art classes, I decided to paint some pictures for the nursery. I ended up picking up canvases, basic paint colors, and brushes for about $40, which was much less than three pictures would have cost! I just did simple sketches of my monster faces onto three canvases, mixed colors to be the same as those in the room, and did some simple painting. Voilà! Custom paintings. How fun, right? And don't be intimidated, this was super easy. Seriously, I may be able to make a mean knitted monster, but I am by no means a painter.

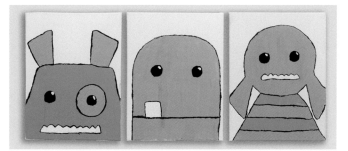

Since I couldn't find the "perfect" monster paintings, I whipped up my own.

SEWING

I ended up making lots of the other items in the nursery just by pulling out my sewing machine and sewing a few simple seams. I picked out some fabrics and made crib sheets, changing-mat covers, crib bumpers, and pillows—all surprisingly simple projects. For the changing table, I bought a basket and made a liner for it out of the same fabrics used elsewhere in the room.

I sewed my own crib bumpers and sheets to get the exact set I wanted.

I couldn't find any monster fabrics, but did you know you can have fabrics custom-printed? Check out the website spoonflower.com, where you can order fabric in your own design. (I threatened to do my own fabrics, but Presley was born before I had a chance to!)

By the end of creating my monster nursery, I had monsters on the brain (umm, even more so than normal?) and was trying to think of everything I could put a monster on. I thought about cutting monsters out of felt and attaching them to my fabric-storage bins with fabric glue. I looked at those sticky lampshades they sell at craft stores and thought about wrapping one in monster fabric. I even added monster decals I found online to a cabinet door and the bookshelves just to monster-ize the furniture. I encourage you to hop on the Internet and explore some of the DIY blogs out there to get ideas for monster-izing your monster nursery!

Keep your eyes peeled for monster things (like these wall decals) and you'll be surprised by what's commercially available!

WALL ART

There's so much you can do to decorate the walls! This is where I really had a blast. I made up some embroidery patterns using images of my monsters, which you can find for free on my blog. I stitched several of them and hung them in their embroidery hoops for a cool wall of monsters.

I found great shelves with lots of little cubbyholes to display little monsters. Get creative! Instead of using the Pocket Blankie (page 48) as a blanket, think about

making your own monster nursery

hanging it on the wall as art. Same goes for the monster swings. I used them to decorate the ceiling, but they would be great as a decoration to hold back curtains, too. Use your imagination, and when in doubt, put a monster on it.

Based on my monster knitting patterns, these embroidery patterns can be downloaded from my blog for free!

Design Tips

- Pick a color scheme and stick with it. You'll notice all of the project samples in this book are in the color scheme I picked for my nursery.

- Customize! It's easier than you think. Cut monsters out of felt and use fabric glue to stick them to store-bought storage bins. Buy a lamp and knit a monster to sit on the base. Hang one of the mini monsters from "Monster Mobile" (page 54) from a doorknob or a curtain tieback. You get the idea!

- Make it art. Think outside the box and hang anything monstery you can find on the walls. Just because it's not designed to be artwork doesn't mean it won't look awesome on the wall! And speaking of boxes, why not buy a shadowbox frame and fill it with monster stuff?

- Keep your eyes peeled for commercially made monster items. I've noticed more and more monster items becoming readily available through large retailers. Just because it doesn't look like something you could use in your nursery at first glance doesn't mean it can't be tweaked, or added to something else to fit in. Appliqués or buttons could be added to lampshades or pillows. Monster-themed scrapbook or wrapping paper could be framed or decoupaged to anything (even furniture). Get creative!

- Have fun. Most importantly, remember that making a special space for a baby should be super fun. Just the fact that you take time to work on a nursery will make your kiddo feel very special as he or she grows older.

Monster Pocket
SWEATER

When I was little, I took a stuffed animal everywhere I went. Since my kiddo fell in love with stuffed creatures at just a couple months old, I figure he's going to follow in my footsteps. With this in mind, I thought it would be practical to design a cute little sweater, great for both boys and girls, with a pocket for a tiny friend. I've also included five patterns in this book for monsters designed to fit perfectly in the pocket of this sweater; turn to "Monster Mobile" on page 54 to check them out.

Skill Level: Intermediate

Sizes: 6 (12, 18) months

Finished Chest: 22½ (24, 26)", including front bands

Finished Length: 13 (14, 15)"

MATERIALS (TO MAKE SWEATER AND MONSTER)

A 2 skeins of Shepherd Sport from Lorna's Laces (100% superwash merino wool; approx 200 yds) in color 13ns Aqua **[2]**

B 2 skeins of Shepherd Sport from Lorna's Laces in color Dusk

C 1 skein of Shepherd Sport from Lorna's Laces in color 54ns Firefly

U.S. size 4 (3.5 mm) 40" circular needle (for Magic Loop method), or size needed to obtain gauge

1 additional needle, straight, circular or double pointed, in same size as circular needle (for 3-needle BO)

Notions: 5 buttons measuring ¾" to 1" in diameter, waste yarn, row counter (optional), 4 stitch markers, tapestry needle, needle and thread (to attach buttons)

GAUGE

24 sts and 32 rows = 4" in St st

SWEATER

Sweater is worked in stripes, alternating 4 rows of A and 4 rows of B.

With A, CO 54 sts. Do not join.

Row 1: K8, PM, K8, PM, K22, PM, K8, PM, K8.

Notes

This hoodie is worked from the top down. A pocket is sewn on at the end, sized perfectly for the mini monsters from "Monster Mobile" starting on page 54.

All slipped sts are slipped pw unless otherwise indicated.

Buttonhole: Work to position of buttonhole, wyif, sl 1, wyib, *sl 1 to right needle, pass second st on right needle over first st as if to BO; rep from * until 5 sts have been bound off. Sl last bound-off st from right needle to left needle. Turn work. Using cable CO, CO 6 sts. Turn work once more. Sl first st on left needle over to right needle and pass second st on right needle over first st to close buttonhole.

Row 2: Purl all sts.

Row 3 (inc row): *Knit to 1 st before marker, K1f&b, sl marker, K1f&b; rep from * 3 more times across row, knit to end.

Row 4: Purl all sts.

Rep rows 3 and 4 a total of 23 (25, 28) times, ending with a WS row. [238 (254, 278) sts]

Switch to C and work in K2, P2 rib for 1". BO all sts in patt.

Sleeves: Place 54 sts from one sleeve onto circular needle. Starting at underarm, PU 1 st from gap between sides, PM to indicate beg of rnd, work arm sts, PU 1 st. [56 (60, 66) sts]

Cont in the rnd using Magic Loop method (page 7) and established stripe patt, work 3 more rnds.

Dec rnd: K2tog, knit to last 2 sts, ssk.

Work dec rnd every 4th rnd until 32 (36, 40) sts rem.

Knit until sleeve has 24 (26, 28) stripes from neck edge.

Switch to C and work in K2, P2 rib for 1".

Loosely BO all sts in patt.

Rep for second sleeve.

HOOD

With B and circular needle, RS facing you, and starting at right neck edge, PU 54 sts around neck. Cont in established stripe patt.

Work 3 rows in St st, ending on a WS row.

Inc row: K1f&b, knit to last 2 sts, K1f&b, K1.

Divide for body and sleeves (RS): Knit to first marker, remove marker, move 54 (58, 64) sleeve sts to waste yarn and remove next marker. Cont knitting across 68 (72, 78) back sts. Remove marker and move next 54 (58, 64) sleeve sts to waste yarn. Remove last marker and knit to end of row. [130 (138, 150) body sts rem]

Cont to work body in established stripe patt until you have 24 (26, 28) total stripes.

Work inc row every RS row, and purl every WS row, until you have 90 (96, 102) sts.

Work until hood has 12 (14, 16) stripes from neck edge.

Divide sts evenly on the 2 needle tips and use additional needle to work 3-needle BO across all sts.

BUTTON BAND

With C, circular needle, RS facing you, and starting at bottom-left edge of sweater, PU 78 (84, 90) sts between bottom edge and neck edge, PM, PU 72 (84, 96) around hood, PM, PU 78 (84, 90) sts from neck to bottom edge. [228 (252, 276) sts] To make picking up sts easier, PU 3 sts per 4-row stripe and

6 sts in the 1" of ribbing.

Work 3 rows in K2, P2 ribbing.

Buttonhole row: On RS, (work buttonhole as described on page 27, work next 12 sts in patt) 4 times, work 1 last buttonhole (you'll have 2 sts left before marker), cont in patt to end of row.

Work 3 more rows in patt.

Loosely BO all sts.

POCKET

With C and circular needle, CO 28 sts. *Do not join.*

Work in K2, P2 rib until pocket measures 4".

Loosely BO all sts in patt.

FINISHING

Weave in all ends. Gently block sweater. Block pocket to 4" x 4". Align bottom edge of pocket with top edge of 3rd stripe from bottom and 1" from front band. Attach pocket using a whipstitch or a running stitch. Line up buttons with buttonholes and use needle and thread to sew buttons onto button band.

Throw your sweater on a kiddo, add a mini monster in the pocket, and you're set for an adventure!

Mini Monsters!

To make a monster the ideal size to fit in that tiny pocket, turn to page 54 for the mini-monster patterns from the "Monster Mobile." I knit up Kevin the Striped Uni-Body Monster (page 60) on U.S. size 2 (2.75 mm) needles in the same yarn I used for the sweater. Perfect fit!

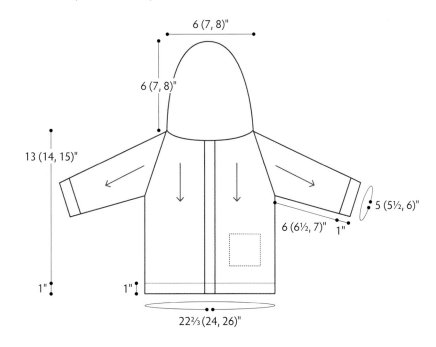

6 (7, 8)"

6 (7, 8)"

13 (14, 15)"

5 (5½, 6)"

6 (6½, 7)" 1"

1" 1"

22⅔ (24, 26)"

Monster
BOOTIES

Baby toes have got to be one of my favorite baby body parts. We see baby toes a lot, since it seems nearly impossible to keep socks on baby feet. But double socking and adding booties on top seemed to do the trick, so of course I made some tiny monster booties. The only thing cuter than baby toes? Baby toes in monster booties.

Skill Level: Intermediate

Sizes: 0-3 (3-6, 6-9) months

Finished Foot Length: 3¾ (4¼, 5)"

MATERIALS

MC 1 skein of Comfort DK from Berroco (50% super fine nylon, 50% super fine acrylic; 50 g/1.75 oz; 178 yds/165 m) in color 2740 Seedling 🅷

CC 1 skein of Comfort DK from Berroco in color 2753 Agean Sea

U.S. size 5 (3.75 mm) 40" circular needle, or size needed to obtain gauge

U.S. size 3 (3.25 mm) needles Notions: Scraps of black and white yarn for face embroidery, row counter (optional), stitch marker, tapestry needle

GAUGE

24 sts and 36 rows: 4" in St st on larger needles

BOOTIES

Slip all sts pw.

Using larger needle and CC, CO 33 (41, 49) sts. *Do not join.*

Rows 1, 3, and 5: Knit all sts.

Row 2: K1, [K1f&b, K13 (17, 21), K1f&b, K1] twice. [37 (45, 53) sts]

Row 4: K1, [K1f&b, K15 (19, 23), K1f&b, K1] twice. [41 (49, 57) sts]

Row 6: K1, [K1f&b, K17 (21, 25), K1f&b, K1] twice. [45 (53, 61) sts]

Baby Rolls

Does your baby have chunky ankles? When working the rib for the cuffs, keep working on the larger needles! My baby had incredibly skinny legs, so no socks or booties ever stayed on, hence the smaller needles for the ribbed cuffs.

Rows 7–10: Knit all sts.

Switch to MC and knit 1 row.

Starting with a purl row, work 9 (13, 17) more rows in St st.

Work short rows to shape toe:

Row 1: K17 (21, 25), ssk, K7, K2tog, sl 1, turn. [43 (51, 59) sts]

Row 2: P2tog, P7, sl 1-P1-psso, sl 1, turn. [41 (49, 57) sts]

Row 3: Ssk, K7, K2tog, sl 1, turn. [39 (47, 55) sts]

Rows 4–9: Work rows 2 and 3 another three more times. [27 (35, 43) sts after row 9]

Row 10: Rep row 2. [25 (33, 41) sts]

Row 11: Ssk, K7, K2tog, knit to end. [23 (31, 39) sts]

Next row: P1, P1f&b, purl to end. [24 (43, 40) sts]

Switch to CC and smaller needles, and knit 1 row.

Work in K1, P1 rib until cuff measures 2 (2½, 2¾)".

Switch to MC and work 1 row in established rib.

BO all sts in patt.

EAR (MAKE 2.)

Using larger needle and CC, CO 8 sts and join, making sure not to twist sts. PM to indicate beg of rnd and beg ear using Magic Loop method (page 7).

Rnd 1: Knit all sts.

Rnd 2: (K1f&b, K3) twice. (10 sts)

Rnd 3: (K4, K1f&b) twice. (12 sts)

Rnd 4: (K1f&b, K5) twice. (14 sts)

Rnd 5: (K6, K1f&b) twice. (16 sts)

Rnds 6–8: Knit all sts.

Divide sts evenly on the 2 needle points and work 3-needle BO to close.

FINISHING

Weave in all ends. Using st-to-st mattress st (right), sew bottom seam on booties. Using row-to-row mattress st (page 35), sew up back seam of booties. Refer to photos for ear placement, and sew ears down using a whipstitch. Use black and white yarn to embroider eyes and mouths, again referring to photos.

Stitch-to-Stitch Mattress Stitch

With RS facing up, thread yarn onto tapestry needle, insert needle under a whole stitch on one side and pull yarn through. Then insert needle under a whole stitch on opposite side and pull yarn through. Continue working from side to side, going into the spot where the previous yarn came out. Gently pull the thread every few stitches to close the seam.

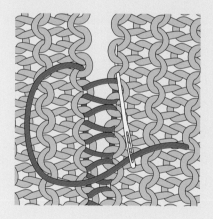

Monster-Face HAT

One of my favorite things to do when my kiddo was a baby was to go out and walk. We started walking when Presley was about three weeks old, and we've walked pretty much every day since. However, because we live in the Northwest, even in the summer I was looking for hats to keep his little head warm. I made this one for him right away, and he wore it all the time. It's just a perfect, easy, go-to kind of hat. I'm sure it will be just the thing for your little monster, too!

Skill Level: Intermediate

Sizes: 6 (12, 18) months

Finished Circumference: 14 (16, 18)"

Finished Height: 6¼ (8, 9)"

MATERIALS

A 1 skein of Comfort from Berroco (50% super fine nylon, 50% super fine acrylic; 100 g/3.5 oz; 210 yds/193 m) in color 9733 Turquoise 🧶

B 1 skein of Comfort from Berroco in color 9714 Robins Egg

C 1 skein of Comfort from Berroco in color 9740 Seedling

U.S. size 8 (5 mm) circular needle, any length, or size needed to obtain gauge

U.S. size 7 (4.5 mm) needles

Scrap of white yarn for tooth

Black shank buttons, 9⁄16"

Notions: Row counter (optional), stitch marker, tapestry needle, needle and thread to attach buttons

GAUGE

20 sts and 26 rows = 4" in St st on larger needle

HAT

With smaller needle and A, CO 60 (72, 80) sts. *Do not join.*

Work back and forth in K1, P1 rib until piece measures 1 (1½, 1½)".

Next row: Switch to larger needle. Cont in established K1, P1 rib, work 22 (28, 32) sts in rib, PM, work 15 sts in rib, PM, work in rib to end.

Switch to B and knit all sts to first marker, work monster-face chart (right) over next 15 sts, switch back to B, knit to end of row.

Using St st and alternating 6 rows in B and 6 rows in A, cont to work chart between st markers. After chart has been worked, work 0 (1, 2) more stripes.

Monster Tip

Yes, this hat is knit flat. If you've ever knit any of my patterns before, I'm sure you realize that I prefer to knit everything in the round. However, colorwork in the round is really not too fun, especially with three colors. So, I decided to write this one to be knit flat, and then seamed. I don't particularly like finishing, but I prefer one quick seam to hitting my head against the wall with colorwork in the round. If you're ambitious, feel free to knit this one in the round.

Shape top:

Row 1: (K2tog, K2) across. [45 (54, 60) sts]

Rows 2 and 4: Purl all sts.

Row 3: (K2tog, K1) across. [30 (36, 40) sts]

Row 5: K2tog across. [15 (18, 20) sts]

Row 6: Cont in same color, P2tog 6 (9, 10) times, P3tog 1 (0, 0) time. [7 (9, 10) sts]

Slide sts back to opposite end of needle so you can start with first st of row. Cut extra-long tail and using tapestry needle, thread through rem sts to close hat and sew up seam.

TOOTH

With top of hat facing upside down, on mouth row, count from edge of monster face to 7th st of the mouth. Beg in 7th st, PU 4 sts in 7th through 4th sts using white yarn.

Knit 6 rows (garter st).

Loosely BO all sts.

FINISHING

Weave in all ends. Use row-to-row mattress st (below) to sew up seam. Sew buttons onto monster face using needle and thread.

Put your hat on a baby.

Row-to-Row Mattress Stitch

With RS facing up, thread tail from top of hat onto tapestry needle, insert needle under one or two bars on one side and pull yarn through. Then insert needle into corresponding bars on the opposite side and pull yarn through. Continue working side to side, gently pulling the thread after every few stitches to close the seam.

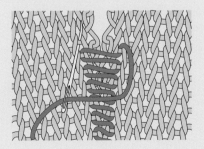

Monster face chart

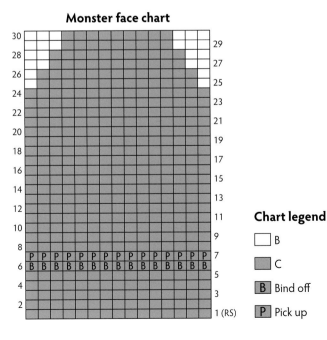

Chart legend

☐	B
▩	C
B	Bind off
P	Pick up

Pointy Monster HAT

Is there anything cuter on a baby than a funny knit hat? I really don't think so. This is such a quick knit, it makes a perfect last-minute baby-shower gift. It's also darling without the eyes and teeth!

Skill Level: Intermediate

Sizes: 6 (12, 18) months

Finished size, not including earflaps or point:

- 6 months: 14" circumference and 5" high
- 12 months: 16" circumference and 6" high
- 18 months: 18½" circumference and 7" high

Note: Model is 10 months and wearing 12-months size.

MATERIALS

For 6-Month Size Shown

1 skein of Shepherd Worsted from Lorna's Laces (100% superwash wool; approx 225 yds) in color 111 Hullabaloo (4)

2 black shank buttons, 9/16" diameter

For 12-Month Size Shown

1 skein of Shepherd Worsted from Lorna's Laces in color 207 Envy
2 black shank buttons, 5/8" diameter

For All Sizes

U.S. size 7 (4.5 mm) 40" circular needle (for Magic Loop method), or size needed to obtain gauge

Scrap of white yarn for teeth

Notions: 2 removable stitch markers, 1 ring stitch marker, stitch holder, row counter (optional), tapestry needle. Optional, if making I-cord ties: 2 double-pointed needles in same size as circular needle

GAUGE

18 sts and 22 rows = 4" in St st

SEED STITCH

Row 1: (K1, P1) across.

Row 2: (P1, K1) across.

Rep rows 1 and 2.

OPTIONAL I-CORD TIES

Using dpns, CO 4 sts onto 1 needle and work as I-cord for 7 (8½, 10)". Transfer these 4 sts to your circular needle and work back and forth beg with row 1 of earflap.

HAT

Beg with earflaps.

Using circular needle, CO 4 sts. *Do not join.*

Row 1: K1f&b, K1, P1, K1f&b. (6 sts)

Row 2: (P1, K1) across.

Row 3: K1f&b, (P1, K1) twice, K1f&b. (8 sts)

Row 4: (K1, P1) across.

Row 5: K1f&b, (K1, P1) 3 times, K1f&b. (10 sts)

Row 6: (P1, K1) across.

Row 7: K1f&b, (P1, K1) 4 times, K1f&b. (12 sts)

Row 8: (K1, P1) across.

Row 9: K1f&b, (K1, P1) 5 times, K1f&b. (14 sts)

Row 10: (P1, K1) across.

6 Months:

Knit 6 more rows even in seed st and place sts on holder. Rep above directions to make 2nd earflap, only this time leave on circular needle.

12 and 18 Months:

Row 11: K1f&b, (P1, K1) 6 times, K1f&b. (16 sts)

Row 12: (K1, P1) across.

12 Months:

Knit 8 more rows even in seed st and place sts on holder. Rep above directions to make 2nd earflap, only this time leave on circular needle.

18 Months:

Row 13: K1f&b, (K1, P1) 7 times, K1f&b. (18 sts)

Row 14: (P1, K1) across.

Knit 10 more rows even in seed st and place sts on holder. Rep above directions to make 2nd earflap, only this time leave on circular needle.

For All Sizes:

Work across 2nd earflap one more time. Turn work and cable CO 16 (20, 24) sts. Turn work back around, place first earflap on left needle and knit across, cont in seed st. Turn again and cable CO 16 (20, 24) more sts.

Divide sts in half for working in the round using Magic Loop method (page 7). Beg to work in the round by pulling out needle tip from last sts worked and joining to first st of first earflap you knit across, PM to indicate beg of rnd. [60 (72, 84) total sts]

First rnd: Work in seed st, place removable marker in first cable CO st after first earflap. Place 2nd removable marker in last cable CO st before 2nd earflap. Work in patt to end of rnd.

Work in seed st until hat measures 1 (1¼, 1½)" from cable CO edge.

Purl 1 rnd.

Switch to St st (knit every rnd) and work until hat measures 3½ (4½, 5½)" from cable CO edge.

Shape top:

Rnd 1: [K2tog, K8 (10, 12)] around. [54 (66, 78) sts]

Rnd 2: Knit all sts.

Rnd 3: [K2tog, K7 (9,11)] around. [48 (60, 72) sts]

Rnd 4: Knit all sts.

Rnd 5: [K2tog, K6 (8, 10)] around. [42 (54, 66) sts]

Rnd 6: Knit all sts.

Rnd 7: [K2tog, K5 (7, 9)] around. [36 (48, 60) sts]

Rnd 8: Knit all sts.

Rnd 9: [K2tog, K4 (6, 8)] around. [30 (42, 54) sts]

Rnd 10: Knit all sts.

Rnd 11: [K2tog, K3 (5, 7)] around. [24 (36, 48) sts]

Rnd 12: Knit all sts.

6 Months:

Rnd 13: (K2tog, K2) around. (18 sts)

Rnds 14 and 15: Knit all sts.

Rnd 16: (K2tog, K1) around. (12 sts)

Rnds 17–19: Knit all sts.

Rnd 20: K2tog around. (6 sts)

Rnds 21 and 22: Knit all sts.

Rnd 23: K2tog, K4. Do not turn. (5 sts)

Slide sts to other end of needle and work 9 rows as an I-cord.

Cut yarn and using tapestry needle, thread through rem sts to finish I-cord.

12 Months:

Rnd 13: (K2tog, K4) around. (30 sts)

Rnd 14: Knit all sts.

Rnd 15: (K2tog, K3) around. (24 sts)

Rnd 16: (K2tog, K2) around. (18 sts)

Rnds 17–19: Knit all sts.

Rnd 20: (K2tog, K1) around. (12 sts)

Rnds 21–23: Knit all sts.

Rnd 24: K2tog around. (6 sts)

Rnds 25 and 26: Knit all sts.

Rnd 27: K2tog, K4. Do not turn. (5 sts)

Slide sts to other end of needle and work 10 rows as an I-cord.

Cut yarn and using tapestry needle, thread through rem sts to finish I-cord.

18 Months:

Rnd 13: (K2tog, K6) around. (42 sts)

Rnd 14: Knit all sts.

Rnd 15: (K2tog, K5) around. (36 sts)

Rnd 16: (K2tog, K4) around. (30 sts)

Rnds 17–19: Knit all sts.

Rnd 20: (K2tog, K3) around. (24 sts)

Rnds 21–23: Knit all sts.

Rnd 24: (K2tog, K2) around. (18 sts)

Rnds 25–27: Knit all sts.

Rnd 28: (K2tog, K1) around. (12 sts)

Rnds 29–31: Knit all sts.

Rnd 32: K2tog around. (6 sts)

Rnds 33 and 34: Knit all sts.

Rnd 35: K2tog, K4. Do not turn. (5 sts)

Slide sts to other end of needle and work 12 rows as an I-cord.

Cut yarn and using tapestry needle, thread through rem sts to finish I-cord.

TOOTH 1

With top of hat facing upside down, count from first removable st marker to 5th (6th, 7th) st from marker. Beg in 5th (6th, 7th) st, PU 5 (6, 7) sts from the purl rnd.

Knit 8 (10, 12) rows (garter st). BO all sts.

TOOTH 2

With top of hat facing upside down, starting in st marked with 2nd removable st marker, PU 5 (6, 7) sts from purl rnd. Work tooth 2 as for tooth 1.

FINISHING

Weave in all ends. Stitch end of I-cord to beg of I-cord to create a loop on top of hat. Use teeth as a guide to sew buttons on for eyes.

Put your hat on your little monster and get outside for a walk!

Monster Safety

I used buttons for eyes on this hat because I just love how they look. Buttons should be used with caution around babies! Be sure to check them regularly to be sure little fingers can't get them off and put them in mouths.

Snuggly Monster
BLANKIE FRIEND

Before I had a baby, I was rather skeptical of all the blanket/stuffed animal things I saw in every baby store I went into. However, once my son, Presley, was born, he was absolutely in love with the things! I wanted to create a special friend perfect for a baby, so I made sure to add in several texture stitches to entertain baby senses. Or in other words, texture stitches perfect for a baby to shove in his mouth!

Skill Level: Intermediate

Finished Size: Approx 13" x 13", not including arms, ears, or feet

MATERIALS

For Black-and-Yellow Monster

MC 1 skein of Shepherd Bulky from Lorna's Laces (100% superwash wool; 140 yds) in color 101 Shadow (5) *(You'll use every last yard of this skein, so you'll need to pull out your gauge swatch if you do it in this color.)*

CC 1 skein of Shepherd Bulky from Lorna's Laces in color 54ns Firefly

For Blue-and-Red Monster

MC 1 skein of Shepherd Bulky from Lorna's Laces in color 407 Devon *(You'll use every last yard of this skein, so you'll need to pull out your gauge swatch if you do it in this color.)*

CC 1 skein of Shepherd Bulky from Lorna's Laces in color Ysolda Red

For Both Monsters

Scrap of black yarn for embroidering eyes and mouth

U.S. size 10½ (6.5 mm) any length circular needle, or size needed to obtain gauge

U.S. size 10 (6 mm) 40" circular needle

Notions: 2 removable stitch markers, row counter (optional), tapestry needle, straight pins (to help with assembly)

GAUGE

13 sts and 24 rows = 4" in double moss st on U.S. size 10½ (6.5 mm) needles

DOUBLE MOSS STITCH

Row 1: (K2, P2) across.

Row 2: (K2, P2) across.

Row 3: (P2, K2) across.

Row 4: (P2, K2) across.

Rep rows 1–4.

BODY

Using size 10½ (6.5 mm) circular needle and MC, CO 44 sts. *Do not join.*

Work in double moss st for 13", or until piece is square.

As you work first row, add removable st markers to st 9 and st 36 to mark 28 middle sts for picking up tummy panel.

BO all sts in patt.

ARM (MAKE 2.)

Using U.S. size 10 (6 mm) circular needle and MC, CO 10 sts and join for working in the rnd using Magic Loop method (page 7), making sure not to twist sts. PM to indicate beg of rnd.

Rnds 1–12: Knit all sts.

Rnd 13: (K1f&b, K4) twice. (12 sts)

Rnds 14 and 15: Knit all sts.

Rnd 16: (K5, K1f&b) twice. (14 sts)

Rnds 17 and 18: Knit all sts.

Rnd 19: (K1f&b, K6) twice. (16 sts)

Rnds 20 and 21: Knit all sts.

Rnd 22: (K7, K1f&b) twice. (18 sts)

Rnds 23 and 24: Knit all sts.

Rnd 25: K2tog around. (9 sts)

Cut yarn and using tapestry needle, thread through rem sts to close hand.

EAR (MAKE 2.)

Using U.S. size 10 (6 mm) circular needle and CC, CO 12 sts and join for working in the rnd using Magic Loop method, making sure not to twist sts. PM to indicate beg of rnd.

Rnd 1: Knit all sts.

Rnd 2: (K1f&b, K5) twice. (14 sts)

Rnd 3: (K6, K1f&b) twice. (16 sts)

Rnd 4: (K1f&b, K7) twice. (18 sts)

Rnd 5: (K8, K1f&b) twice. (20 sts)

Rnd 6: (K1f&b, K9) twice. (22 sts)

Rnd 7: (K10, K1f&b) twice. (24 sts)

Rnds 8–16: Knit all sts.

Turn ear inside out, divide sts evenly on the 2 needle tips, and work 3-needle BO on all sts (smaller size needle will work fine).

FOOT (MAKE 2.)

Using U.S. size 10 (6 mm) circular needle and CC, CO 14 sts and join for working in the rnd using Magic Loop method, making sure not to twist sts. PM to indicate beg of rnd.

Rnd 1: Knit all sts.

Rnd 2: (K1f&b, K6) twice. (16 sts)

Rnd 3: (K7, K1f&b) twice. (18 sts)

Rnd 4: (K1f&b, K8) twice. (20 sts)

Rnd 5: (K9, K1f&b) twice. (22 sts)

Rnds 6–15: Knit all sts.

Rnd 16: (Ssk, K7, K2tog) twice. (18 sts)

Rnd 17: (Ssk, K5, K2tog) twice. (14 sts)

Rnd 18: (Ssk, K3, K2tog) twice. (10 sts)

Cut yarn and use tapestry needle to pull it through rem sts and close foot.

EYE PATCH

Using U.S. size 10 (6 mm) circular needle and CC, CO 6 sts and join for working in the rnd using Magic Loop method, making sure not to twist sts. PM to indicate beg of rnd.

Rnd 1: K1f&b all sts. (12 sts)

Rnd 2: (K1f&b, K1) around. (18 sts)

Rnd 3: (K1f&b, K2) around. (24 sts)

Rnd 4: (K1f&b, K3) around. (30 sts)

Rnd 5: (K1f&b, K4) around. (36 sts)

Rnd 6: (K1f&b, K5) around. (42 sts)

Rnd 7: (K1f&b, K6) around. (48 sts)

Rnds 8 and 9: Knit all sts.

Rnd 10: BO all sts.

TUMMY

With marker side facing up and using U.S. size 10 (6 mm) needle and CC, PU 28 sts between the 2 markers from first row.

Work in K2, P2 rib for 4".

Dec row: Ssk, work sts as they appear (knit the knits and purl the purls) until you have 2 sts left, K2tog.

Work dec row every row until 12 sts rem.

Loosely BO all sts in patt.

FINISHING

Weave in all ends. Pin down sides and top of tummy panel and use a running stitch to sew it to body. If you want, you can add a bit of stuffing to make the tummy stand out; stitch around most of the tummy panel and add a bit of fluff in when you have about 2" to 3" on one side still open, and then finish sewing.

Turn to "Monster-Making University" on page 15 for detailed finishing directions. Use straight pins and the photos for reference to play around with the placement of the arms, ears, feet, and eye patch. Use a whipstitch to attach the ears to the top of the body, the feet to the bottom, and the arms to the sides. Use a running st around the eye patch. To embroider the face, use a satin st to make an oval eye shape, and a running st to make a smile.

Hand your blanket friend to a small person, but don't be surprised if it's immediately in his or her mouth.

Cuddly Monster BLANKIE

Who doesn't want to nuzzle a snuggly monster? The cozy cotton yarn makes this blanket perfect for cuddling when it's cold out, or even wrapping up little ones right out of the bath. Plus, with built-in hands and ears perfectly sized for little hands, this blanket is extra easy for a kiddo to drag around! Just make sure to sew those hands on extra securely.

Skill Level: Intermediate

Finished Size: Approx 36" x 36", not including hands or ears

MATERIALS

For Blue-and-Gray Blanket

MC 7 balls of Comfy Worsted from Knit Picks (75% pima cotton, 25% acrylic; 50 g/109 yds) in color B981 Sea Foam ⓘ4ⓘ

CC 6 balls of Comfy Worsted from Knit Picks in color K238 Hawk

For Green-and-White Blanket

MC 7 balls of Comfy Worsted from Knit Picks in color 6315 Peapod

CC 6 balls of Comfy Worsted from Knit Picks in color 9437 White

For Both Blankets

Scrap of white yarn for teeth in same weight and fiber as project yarn

Scrap of black yarn for eyes in same weight and fiber as project yarn

U.S. size 7 (4.5 mm) 40" circular needle, or size needed to obtain gauge

1 additional needle, straight, circular, or double pointed, in same size as circular needle (for 3-needle BO)

Notions: Stitch marker, row counter (optional), tapestry needle, stitch holders, small amount of stuffing

GAUGE

18 sts and 24 rows = 4" in St st

BLANKET

Blanket is worked in stripes, alternating 4 rows in MC and 4 rows in CC.

With MC, CO 4 sts. *Do not join.*

Knit 1 row.

Inc row: K1, K1f&b, knit to end.

Working in stripe patt, rep inc row every row until you have 195 sts. You'll end on 4th row of a CC stripe.

Knit next 12 rows even in established stripe patt.

Dec row: K1, K2tog, knit to end.

Cont in stripe patt, rep dec row every row until 4 sts rem.

Loosely BO all sts.

HOOD

Using circular needle and MC, CO 4 sts. *Do not join.* Cont in established stripe patt.

Knit 1 row.

Inc row: K1, K1f&b, knit to end.

Working in established stripe patt, rep inc row until you have 79 sts. You'll end on 4th row of a MC stripe.

Loosely BO all sts.

HAND (MAKE 2.)

The hands are knit entirely in MC.

Using circular needle and MC, CO 18 sts pgs 42, 46, 50, 57, 78, 83, 105 and join for working in the rnd using Magic Loop method (page 7), making sure not to twist sts. PM to indicate beg of rnd.

Rnd 1: Knit all sts.

Rnd 2: (K1f&b, K7, K1f&b) twice. (22 sts)

Rnd 3: Knit all sts.

Rnd 4: (K1f&b, K9, K1f&b) twice. (26 sts)

Rnd 5: Knit all sts.

Rnd 6: (K1f&b, K11, K1f&b) twice. (30 sts)

Rnd 7: Knit all sts.

Rnd 8: (K1f&b, K13, K1f&b) twice. (34 sts)

Rnd 9: Knit all sts.

Rnd 10: (K1f&b, K15, K1f&b) twice. (38 sts)

Rnd 11: Knit all sts.

Rnd 12: (K1f&b, K17, K1f&b) twice. (42 sts)

Rnd 13: Knit all sts.

Rnd 14: (K1f&b, K19, K1f&b) twice. (46 sts)

Rnd 15: Knit all sts.

Rnd 16: (K1f&b, K21, K1f&b) twice. (50 sts)

Rnd 17: Knit all sts.

Rnd 18: (K1f&b, K23, K1f&b) twice. (54 sts)

Rnds 19–24: Knit all sts.

Rnd 25: K9, place next 36 sts on holders or waste yarn to be worked later.

Finger 1

Rejoin new rnd by knitting across gap and working last 9 sts of rnd. The first 9 and last 9 sts of the original hand rnd will be your new rnd. This completes rnd 1 of first finger. (18 sts total)

Knit 7 rnds using Magic Loop method.

Next rnd: K2tog around. (9 sts)

Cut yarn and using tapestry needle, thread through rem sts to close finger.

Finger 2

Move first 9 and last 9 sts from holder to needles. (18 sts total)

Rejoin working yarn and knit 8 rnds using Magic Loop method.

Next rnd: K2tog around. (9 sts)

Cut yarn and using tapestry needle, thread through rem sts to close finger.

Finger 3

Move last 18 sts from holder to needles.

Rejoin working yarn and knit 8 rnds using Magic Loop method.

Next rnd: K2tog around. (9 sts)

Cut yarn and using tapestry needle, thread through rem sts to close last finger.

EAR (MAKE 2.)

The ears are knit entirely in MC.

Using circular needle and MC, CO 16 sts and join for working in the rnd using Magic Loop method, making sure not to twist sts. PM to indicate beg of rnd.

Rnd 1: Knit all sts.

Rnd 2: (K1f&b, K7) twice. (18 sts)

Rnd 3: Knit all sts.

Rnd 4: (K8, K1f&b) twice. (20 sts)

Rnd 5: Knit all sts.

Rnd 6: (K1f&b, K9) twice. (22 sts)

Rnd 7: Knit all sts.

Rnd 8: (K10, K1f&b) twice. (24 sts)

Rnd 9: Knit all sts.

Rnd 10: (K1f&b, K11) twice. (26 sts)

Rnd 11: Knit all sts.

Rnd 12: (K12, K1f&b) twice. (28 sts)

Rnd 13: Knit all sts.

Rnd 14: (K1f&b, K13) twice. (30 sts)

Rnd 15: Knit all sts.

Rnd 16: (K14, K1f&b) twice. (32 sts)

Rnd 17: Knit all sts.

Rnd 18: (K1f&b, K15) twice. (34 sts)

Rnd 19: Knit all sts.

Rnd 20: (K16, K1f&b) twice. (36 sts)

Rnd 21: Knit all sts.

Rnd 22: (K1f&b, K17) twice. (38 sts)

Rnd 23: Knit all sts.

Rnd 24: (K18, K1f&b) twice. (40 sts)

Rnd 25: Knit all sts.

Rnd 26: (K1f&b, K19) twice. (42 sts)

Rnd 27: Knit all sts.

Rnd 28: (K20, K1f&b) twice. (44 sts)

Rnds 29–35: Knit all sts.

Evenly divide sts on the 2 needle tips and work 3-needle BO to close.

EYE (MAKE 2.)

Using circular needle and black, CO 4 sts and join for working in the rnd using Magic Loop method, making sure not to twist sts. PM to indicate beg of rnd.

Rnd 1: K1f&b all sts. (8 sts)

Rnd 2: (K1f&b, K1) around. (12 sts)

Rnd 3: (K1f&b, K1) around. (18 sts)

Rnd 4: Knit all sts.

Rnd 5: BO all sts.

TOOTH (MAKE 5.)

Using circular needle and white, CO 12 sts and join for working in the rnd using Magic Loop method, making sure not to twist sts. PM to indicate beg of rnd.

Rnds 1–6: Knit all sts.

Evenly divide sts on the 2 needle tips and work 3-needle BO to close.

FINISHING

Weave in ends and lightly block as needed. Close up any holes between fingers and stuff hand. Use a whip-stitch to attach hands to corners that are not BO or CO. Use running st to sew hood RS up onto WS of blanket on BO or CO corner. Use running st around eyes to attach them to hood. Whipstitch teeth onto bound-off edge of hood. Whipstitch ears to sides of hood. Refer to "Monster-Making University" (page 15) for detailed monster-finishing directions.

Wrap this blanket around your favorite little monster!

cuddly monster blankie

Pocket Blankie with MONSTER FRIEND

We sure did use a lot of blankets when Presley was little, but the unique ones were used most. I designed this one as sort of half-toy, half-blanket. Babies love stripes! At just a month old Presley was fascinated by the gray-and-black stripes. This blanket is fun to hang on the edge of a crib or to use as a stroller blanket since the monster can be moved into different pockets for entertainment.

Knit the monster given here, or substitute any of the monsters from "Monster Mobile" (page 54). Just use the same yarn for the blanket and a U.S. size 5 needle.

Skill Level: Intermediate

Finished Size:

- Blanket: Approx 35" x 36"
- Monster: Approx 11" tall

MATERIALS (TO MAKE BLANKET AND MONSTER)

A 2 skeins of Sweater from Spud & Chloë (55% wool, 45% organic cotton; 100 g; 160 yds/146 m) in color 7502 Grass (4)

B 2 skeins of Sweater from Spud & Chloë in color 7521 Beluga

C 2 skeins of Sweater from Spud & Chloë in color 7522 Penguin

D 1 skein of Sweater from Spud & Chloë in color 7510 Splash

E 1 skein of Sweater from Spud & Chloë in color 7507 Moonlight

U.S. size 9 (5.5 mm) 40" or longer circular needle, or size needed to obtain gauge

1 additional needle, straight, circular, or double pointed, in same size as circular needle (for 3-needle BO)

Notions: Stuffing, row counter (optional), stitch marker, tapestry needle, straight pins (to help with assembly)

GAUGE

16 sts and 20 rows = 4" in St st

BLANKET

Using circular needle and A, CO 144. *Do not join.*

Row 1: K1, K2tog, *P1, K1; rep from * to last 3 sts, P2tog, K1. (142 sts)

Rows 2–12: Rep row 1. You'll have 120 sts at end of row 12.

Row 13: Switch to B and knit all sts.

Row 14: Purl all sts.

Cont in St st, alternating 8 rows B and 8 rows C, until you have 21 stripes.

Switch back to A.

Edge row: K1, K1f&b, *K1, P1; rep from * to last 2 sts, K1f&b, K1.

Rep edge row until you have 144 sts.

Loosely BO all sts.

Work side borders:

Row 1: With RS facing you and beg at bottom-right corner stripe, PU approx 120 sts along stripe edge of blanket. The number of sts you end up with is not really important. The rule of thumb is to PU 2 sts per 3 rows. Just be sure to have an even number of sts.

Rows 2–13: K1, K1f&b, *K1, P1; rep from * to last 2 sts, K1f&b, K1.

Row 14: BO all sts loosely on WS. Rep on other side of blanket to complete border. Sew mitered corners tog.

Monster Tip

I carry the yarn up the side, wrapping one color around another every other row. You'll never see it in the end, thanks to picking up the edging. And the fewer ends to weave in at the end, the better!

POCKETS

Make one of each like I did, or all four matching to suit your taste.

STOCKINETTE STRIPED POCKET

Using circular needle and A, CO 37 sts. *Do not join.*

Knit 2 rows.

Switch to D and knit 2 rows.

Cont alternating 2 rows A and 2 rows D until piece measures 8½".

With D, work K1, P1 rib until pocket measures 9".

Loosely BO all sts in patt.

BLUE-AND-BLUE WAVES POCKET

Using circular needle and D, CO 37 sts. *Do not join.*

Work 2 rows in St st.

Switch to E.

Row 1: (K1, sl 3 wyib) across, ending K1.

Row 2: P2, (sl 1 wyif, P3) across, ending last rep P2.

Row 3: Knit all sts.

Row 4: Purl all sts.

Switch to D and work rows 1–4 once more.

Rep rows 1–4, switching between D and E every 4 rows, until pocket measures 9".

Loosely BO all sts.

DIAGONAL-STRIPES POCKET

Using circular needle and E, CO 4 sts. *Do not join.*

Knit 1 row.

Inc row: K1f&b, knit to end.

Rep inc row, switching between E and D on every 4th row until you have 53 sts, or until piece measures 9" when measured along a straight edge.

Dec row: K1, K2tog, knit to end.

Cont in 4-row stripe patt, rep dec row until you have 4 sts left.

Loosely BO all sts.

WINDOWPANE POCKET

Using circular needle and E, CO 37 sts. *Do not join.*

Knit 2 rows.

Switch to A.

Row 1: K2, (sl 1 wyib, K3) across, ending last rep K2.

Row 2: P2, (sl 1 wyif, P3) across, ending last rep P2.

Rows 3 and 4: Rep rows 1 and 2.

Rows 5 and 6: Using E, knit all sts.

Rep rows 1–6 until pocket measures 9", ending on row 6.

Loosely BO all sts.

MONSTER

Using circular needle and E, CO 36 sts and join for working in the rnd using Magic Loop method (page 7), making sure not to twist sts. PM to indicate beg of rnd.

Rnds 1–21: Work 3 rnds E and 3 rnds D for a total of 7 stripes.

Rnds 22–33: Switch to A and knit all sts. Cont with A to end.

Rnd 34: (Ssk, K14, K2tog) twice. (32 sts)

Rnd 35: (Ssk, K12, K2tog) twice. (28 sts)

Turn body inside out, divide sts evenly on the 2 needle tips, and work 3-needle BO on all sts. Turn body RS out.

ARM (MAKE 2.)

Using circular needle and D, CO 8 sts and join for working in the rnd using Magic Loop method, making sure not to twist sts. PM to indicate beg of rnd.

Rnds 1–15: Knit all sts.

Rnds 16–20: Switch to A and knit all sts. Cont with A to end.

Rnd 21: K2tog around. (4 sts)

Cut yarn and using tapestry needle, thread through rem sts to close hand.

LEG (MAKE 2.)

Using circular needle and E, CO 10 sts and join for working in the rnd using Magic Loop method, making sure not to twist sts. PM to indicate beg of rnd.

Rnds 1–20: Knit all sts.

Switch to A. Cont with A to end.

Rnd 21: K4, K1f&b, K1f&b, K4. (12 sts)

Rnd 22: K5, K1f&b, K1f&b, K5. (14 sts)

pocket blankie with monster friend

Rnd 23: K6, K1f&b, K1f&b, K6. (16 sts)

Rnd 24: K7, K1f&b, K1f&b, K7. (18 sts)

Rnds 25–29: Knit all sts.

Rnd 30: (K2tog, K5, K2tog) twice. (14 sts)

Cut yarn leaving an 18" tail. Use tapestry needle and Kitchener st to close foot.

EAR (MAKE 2.)

Using circular needle and A, CO 5 sts. *Do not join.*

Row 1: K1, P1, end K1.

Row 2: Rep row 1.

Row 3: K1f&b, (P1, K1) to end. (6 sts)

Row 4: K1f&b, (P1, K1) across, ending P1. (7 sts)

Rows 5–8: (P1, K1) across, ending P1.

Row 9: Ssk, (P1, K1) across, ending P1. (6 sts)

Row 10: (P1, K1) to end.

Row 11: (K1, P1) twice, K2tog. (5 sts)

Row 12: (K1, P1) across, ending K1.

Row 13: Ssk, K1, P1, K1. (4 sts)

Row 14: (K1, P1) twice.

Row 15: P1, K1, K2tog. (3 sts)

Row 16: P1, K1, P1.

Row 17: Ssk, P1. (2 sts)

Cut yarn and using tapestry needle, thread through rem sts to close ear.

FINISHING

Weave in all ends. Block pockets to 9" x 9". Once blocked, use diagram to line up pockets, and attach them to blanket using a whipstitch. Block blanket to 35" wide x 36" long.

Stuff feet, body, and hands of monster. Using photos for reference, embroider eyes and mouth.

Whipstitch arms to sides of body and ears to top of head. Use a running st to attach legs to inside of bottom edge of body, and then to sew bottom seam shut.

For more detailed monster-finishing information, turn to "Monster-Making University" on page 15.

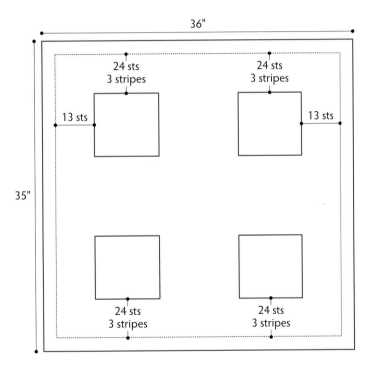

pocket blankie with monster friend

Monster
MOBILE

What nursery is complete without a mobile above the crib? I wanted something truly outstanding for my monster nursery, and my son, Presley, thinks this mobile is pretty amazing. I'd set up a small fan on the floor and point it at the mobile to get it to spin, and he'd stare at it for hours. You can also use a commercial mobile for the musical spinner or check Christmas shops for an ornament rotator. Once it's no longer needed above a crib, this mobile looks fantastic hanging anywhere in your kiddo's room.

Skill Level: Intermediate

Finished Size: Approx 14" diameter

20" drop from hanger to top of ring

Lowest monster hangs 12.5" from ring.

MATERIALS

A 1 skein of Heritage from Cascade Yarns (75% superwash merino, 25% nylon; 100 g/3.5 oz; 437 yds/400 m) in color 5655 Como Blue **1**

B 1 skein of Heritage from Cascade Yarns in color 5618 Snow

C 1 skein of Heritage from Cascade Yarns in color 5660 Grey

D 1 skein of Heritage from Cascade Yarns in color 5630 Anis

E 1 skein of Heritage from Cascade Yarns in color 5652 Mustard

U.S. size 1 (2.25 mm) 40" circular needle (for Magic Loop method)

Set of U.S. size 1 (2.25 mm) double-pointed needles, or size needed to obtain gauge

Set of U.S. size 2 (2.75 mm) double-pointed needles

5 pairs of 6 mm black safety eyes

Scraps of black and white yarn for face embroidery, or white felt and fabric glue

14"-diameter wooden or plastic embroidery hoop (you'll only use the inside ring)

Notions: Stuffing, row counter (optional), stitch marker, tapestry needle, straight pins (for assembling), fishing swivel and monofilament (for hanging)

GAUGE

32 sts and 44 rows = 4" in St st on smaller needles

RING COVER

Using 2 strands of A held tog, CO 12 sts onto 1 larger dpn. *Do not join.*

Working in St st, alternate 4 rows A and 4 rows B until piece measures 45½", ending on a B stripe.

Loosely BO all sts.

MOBILE HANGER

Using larger dpns and 2 strands of A held tog, use provisional CO (page 9) to CO 4 sts onto 1 dpn.

Knit as an I-cord (page 56) for 4".

Making a loop with your I-cord, transfer the 4 provisional CO sts onto needle. Knit across all 8 sts.

Cont as an I-cord, K2tog all sts of next row. (4 sts)

Cont I-cord until it measures 6" from top of loop (or length desired for your mobile).

I-Cord

"Monster Mobile" (page 54) and "Monster Swings" (page 64) include a lot of I-cord. The "I" in I-cord stands for "idiot." Yes, it's that simple to make. Cast on the required number of stitches onto a double-pointed needle. *Knit the stitches. Then, do not turn your work, but slide the stitches back to the right end of the needle. Repeat from * until I-cord is the desired length.

Switch to C and beg ball, working in the round instead of an I-cord.

Rnd 1: K1f&b all sts, dividing sts to 3 needles as you go. (8 sts)

Rnd 2: K1f&b all sts. (16 sts)

Rnd 3: (K1f&b, K1) around. (24 sts)

Rnd 4: (K1f&b, K2) around. (32 sts)

Rnds 5–14: Knit all sts.

Rnd 15: (K2tog, K2) around. (24 sts)

Rnd 16: (K2tog, K1) around. (16 sts)

Stuff ball now.

Rnd 17: K2tog around. (8 sts)

Cut yarn and using tapestry needle, thread through rem sts to close ball.

HANGING SPOKE

(Make 5: 2 with B ball, 1 with C ball, 1 with D ball, 1 with E ball.)

Using larger dpns and 2 strands of A held tog, CO 4 sts onto 1 dpn.

Knit as an I-cord for 4".

Switch to 2 strands held tog of ball color.

Beg working in the round instead of an I-cord.

Rnd 1: K1f&b all sts, dividing sts to 3 needles as you go. (8 sts)

Rnd 2: K1f&b all sts. (16 sts)

Rnds 3–10: Knit all sts.

Rnd 11: K2tog around. (8 sts)

Stuff and switch back to 2 strands of A held tog.

Rnd 12: K2tog around. (4 sts)

Switch back to 1 needle and knit as an I-cord for 2" more.

Cut yarn and tapestry needle, thread through rem sts to close spoke.

DANGLE

(Make 15: 5 in C, 5 in D, 5 in E.)

Using smaller dpns and 1 strand of desired dangle color, CO 3 sts onto 1 dpn.

Rnds 1–4: Knit as an I-cord.

Rnd 5: K1f&b all sts, dividing sts to 3 needles as you go. (6 sts)

Rnd 6: K1f&b all sts. (12 sts)

Rnd 7: (K1f&b, K1) around. (18 sts)

Rnds 8–14: Knit all sts.

Rnd 15: K2tog around. (9 sts)

Rnd 16: K2tog around, ending K1. (5 sts)

Cut yarn, stuff dangle, and using tapestry needle, thread through rem sts to close dangle.

SWING (MAKE 5.)

Using larger dpns and 2 strands of B held tog, CO 4 sts onto 1 dpn.

Knit as an I-cord for 13".

Cut yarn and using tapestry needle, thread through rem sts to close I-cord.

LLOYD THE TALL MONSTER

Finished size: 6½" tall

Use1 strand of A on U.S. size 1 (2.25 mm) needles to knit the tall monster.

BODY

Using circular needle, CO 32 sts and join for working in the rnd using Magic Loop method (page 7), making sure not to twist sts. PM to indicate beg of rnd.

Rnds 1–45: Knit all sts.

Rnd 46: (K2tog, K12, K2tog) twice. (28 sts)

Rnd 47: (K2tog, K10, K2tog) twice. (24 sts)

Rnd 48: (K2tog, K8, K2tog) twice. (20 sts)

Rnd 49: (K2tog, K6, K2tog) twice. (16 sts)

Turn monster body inside out, divide sts evenly on the 2 needle tips, and work 3-needle BO on all sts. Turn monster body RS out.

ARM (MAKE 2.)

Using circular needle, CO 10 sts and join for working in the rnd using Magic Loop method, making sure not to twist sts. PM to indicate beg of rnd.

Rnds 1–35: Knit all sts.

Rnd 36: K2tog around. (5 sts)

Cut yarn and using tapestry needle, thread through rem sts to close hand.

LEG (MAKE 2.)

Using circular needle, CO 10 sts and join for working in the rnd using Magic Loop method, making sure not to twist sts. PM to indicate beg of rnd.

Rnds 1–35: Knit all sts.

Rnd 36: K3, K1f&b 4 times, K3. (14 sts)

Rnd 37: K5, K1f&b 4 times, K5. (18 sts)

Rnd 38: K8, K1f&b twice, K8. (20 sts)

Rnd 39: K9, K1f&b twice, K9. (22 sts)

Rnds 40–44: Knit all sts.

Rnd 45: (Ssk, K7, K2tog) twice. (18 sts)

Stuff foot. Cut yarn, leaving long tail. Using tapestry needle, work Kitchener st on all sts to close foot.

FLOYD THE TOOTHY MONSTER

Finished size: 6½" tall

Use 1 strand of E on U.S. size 1 (2.25 mm) needles to knit the toothy monster.

BODY

Using circular needle, CO 36 sts and join for working in the rnd using Magic Loop method, making sure not to twist sts. PM to indicate beg of rnd.

Rnds 1–24: Knit all sts.

Rnd 25: BO first 18 sts of rnd, knit to end. (18 sts)

Rnd 26: PU through back loop only the 18 sts you bound off in last rnd. Knit to end. (36 sts) *These 2 rnds will make up a ridge that creates the mouth.*

Rnds 27–35: Knit all sts.

Rnd 36: (Ssk, K14, K2tog) twice. (32 sts)

Rnd 37: (Ssk, K12, K2tog) twice. (28 sts)

Rnd 38: (Ssk, K10, K2tog) twice. (24 sts)

Turn monster body inside out, divide sts evenly on the 2 needle tips, and work 3-needle BO on all sts. Turn monster body RS out.

ARM (MAKE 2.)

Using circular needle, CO 8 sts and join for working in the rnd using Magic Loop method, making sure not to twist sts. PM to indicate beg of rnd.

Rnds 1–24: Knit all sts.

Rnd 25: K1f&b 5 times, K3. (13 sts)

Rnds 26–33: Knit all sts.

Rnd 34: K2tog 6 times, end K1. (7 sts)

Stuff hand. Cut yarn and using tapestry needle, thread through rem sts to close hand.

LEG (MAKE 2.)

Using circular needle, CO 10 sts and join for working in the rnd using Magic Loop method, making sure not to twist sts. PM to indicate beg of rnd.

Rnds 1–35: Knit all sts. At end of rnd 35, TURN.

Working on only last 5 sts of rnd:

Row 1: Sl 1, purl to end.

Row 2: Sl 1, knit to end.

Work rows 1 and 2 for 5 rows, ending on a purl row.

Rnd 1 of foot: Turn once again, PM, this will become your new beg of rnd. Knit across heel sts once more. Using same needle tip, PU 3 sts from left-hand side of heel flap. Flip to other needle tip and knit across held instep sts and PU 3 sts from right-hand side of heel flap. (16 sts)

Rnd 2: K5, K2tog, K7, K2tog. (14 sts)

Rnds 3–11: Knit all sts.

Rnd 12: K2tog around. (7 sts)

Stuff foot. Cut yarn and using tapestry needle, thread through rem sts to close foot.

TOOTH

With head facing down, starting on 8th st, and using scrap white yarn, PU 4 sts through just the back st on bound-off row of mouth.

Rnds 1–5: Knit all sts.

Rnd 6: BO all sts in patt.

CHARLOTTE THE BLUE-AND-AQUA MONSTER

Finished size: 4" tall

Use 1 strand of C for body and 1 strand of A for feet and ears on U.S. size 1 (2.25 mm) needles to knit the blue-and-aqua monster.

BODY

Using circular needle and C, CO 44 sts and join for working in the rnd using Magic Loop method, making sure not to twist sts. PM to indicate beg of rnd.

Rnds 1–20: Knit all sts.

Rnd 21: (K2tog, K20) twice. (42 sts)

Rnd 22: Knit all sts.

Rnd 23: (K19, K2tog) twice. (40 sts)

Rnd 24: Knit all sts.

Rnd 25: (K2tog, K18) twice. (38 sts)

Rnd 26: Knit all sts.

Rnd 27: (K17, K2tog) twice. (36 sts)

Rnd 28: Knit all sts.

Rnd 29: (K2tog, K16) twice. (34 sts)

Rnd 30: Knit all sts.

Rnd 31: (K15, K2tog) twice. (32 sts)

Rnd 32: (Ssk, K12, K2tog) twice. (28 sts)

Rnd 33: (Ssk, K10, K2tog) twice. (24 sts)

Rnd 34: (Ssk, K8, K2tog) twice. (20 sts)

Turn monster body inside out, divide sts evenly on the 2 needle tips, and work 3-needle BO on all sts. Turn monster body RS out.

ARM (MAKE 2.)

Using circular needle and C, CO 10 sts and join for working in the rnd using Magic Loop method, making sure not to twist sts. PM to indicate beg of rnd.

Rnds 1–23: Knit all sts.

Rnd 24: K2tog around. (5 sts)

Cut yarn and using tapestry needle, thread through rem sts to close hand.

FOOT (MAKE 2.)

Using circular needle and A, CO 10 sts and join for working in the rnd using Magic Loop method, making sure not to twist sts. PM to indicate beg of rnd.

Rnd 1: Knit all sts.

Rnd 2: (K1f&b, K4) twice. (12 sts)

Rnd 3: (K5, K1f&b) twice. (14 sts)

Rnd 4: (K1f&b, K6) twice. (16 sts)

Rnd 5: (K7, K1f&b) twice. (18 sts)

Rnds 6–12: Knit all sts.

Rnd 13: (Ssk, K5, K2tog) twice. (14 sts)

Rnd 14: (Ssk, K3, K2tog) twice. (10 sts)

Cut yarn, leaving long tail. Using tapestry needle, work Kitchener st on all sts to close foot.

EAR (MAKE 2.)

Using circular needle and A, CO 8 sts and join for working in the rnd using Magic Loop method, making sure not to twist sts. PM to indicate beg of rnd.

Rnd 1: Knit all sts.

Rnd 2: (K1f&b, K3) twice. (10 sts)

Rnd 3: Knit all sts.

Rnd 4: (K4, K1f&b) twice. (12 sts)

Rnds 5–10: Knit all sts.

Divide sts evenly on the 2 needle tips and work 3-needle BO across sts to close ear.

Work leg in stripes, alternating 3 rnds D and 3 rnds B.

Rnd 1: K1f&b all sts. (12 sts)

Rnd 2: (K1f&b, K1) around. (18 sts)

Rnds 3–18: Knit all sts. At end of rnd 18, use backward-loop CO (page 13) to CO 2 sts and cut yarn. (20 sts)

Following directions in "Legs to Body" on page 15, transfer leg sts to circular needle as follows. For first leg, put 9 sts on front needle and 11 sts (9 leg sts plus 2 CO sts) on back needle. For second leg, again make sure to cut your yarn, and put 11 sts (9 leg sts plus 2 CO sts) on front needle and 9 sts on back needle. You'll have 40 sts total and a new beg of rnd in middle of Kevin's second leg.

BODY

Cont in established stripe patt, PM to indicate beg of rnd and using Magic Loop method, attach yarn and beg body.

Rnds 1–24: Knit all sts.

Rnd 25: (K2tog, K18) twice. (38 sts)

Rnd 26: Knit all sts.

Rnd 27: (K17, K2tog) twice. (36 sts)

Rnd 28: Knit all sts.

Rnd 29: (K2tog, K16) twice. (34 sts)

Rnd 30: Knit all sts.

Rnd 31: (K15, K2tog) twice. (32 sts)

Rnd 32: Knit all sts.

Rnd 33: (K2tog, K14) twice. (30 sts)

Rnd 34: Knit all sts.

Rnd 35: (K13, K2tog) twice. (28 sts)

Rnd 36: (Ssk, K10, K2tog) twice. (24 sts)

Rnd 37: (Ssk, K8, K2tog) twice. (20 sts)

Rnd 38: (Ssk, K6, K2tog) twice. (16 sts)

Turn monster body inside out, divide sts evenly on the 2 needle tips, and work 3-needle BO on all sts. Turn monster body RS out.

ARM (MAKE 2.)

Using circular needle and D, CO 12 sts and join for working in the rnd using Magic Loop method, making sure not to twist sts. PM to indicate beg of rnd.

Rnds 1–33: Knit all sts, alternating 3 rnds D and 3 rnds B.

Rnd 34: Cont with B, K2tog around. (6 sts)

Cut yarn and using tapestry needle, thread through rem sts to close hand.

KEVIN THE STRIPED UNI-BODY MONSTER

Finished size: 4" tall

Use 1 strand of D and 1 strand of B on U.S. size 1 (2.25 mm) needles to knit the uni-body monster.

LEG (MAKE 2.)

Using circular needle and D, CO 6 sts and join for working in the rnd using Magic Loop method, making sure not to twist sts. PM to indicate beg of rnd.

DEREK THE SHORT SQUARE MONSTER

Finished size: 4" tall

Use 1 strand of E and 1 strand of C on U.S. size 1 (2.25 mm) needles to knit the short square monster.

BODY

Using circular needle and C, CO 48 sts and join for working in the rnd using Magic Loop method, making sure not to twist sts. PM to indicate beg of rnd.

Rnds 1–10: Knit all sts, alternating 2 rnds C and 2 rnds E.

Rnds 11–19: Switch to MC, knit all sts.

Rnd 20: (Ssk, K20, K2tog) twice. (44 sts)

Rnd 21: (Ssk, K18, K2tog) twice. (40 sts)

Rnd 22: (Ssk, K16, K2tog) twice. (36 sts)

Turn monster body inside out, divide sts evenly on the 2 needle tips, and work 3-needle BO on all sts. Turn monster body RS out.

ARM (MAKE 2.)

Using circular needle and MC, CO 8 sts and join for working in the rnd using Magic Loop method, making sure not to twist sts. PM to indicate beg of rnd.

Rnds 1–18: Knit all sts.

Cut yarn and using tapestry needle, thread through rem sts to close hand.

LEG (MAKE 2.)

Using circular needle and E, CO 10 sts and join for working in the rnd using Magic Loop method, making sure not to twist sts. PM to indicate beg of rnd.

Rnds 1–20: Knit all sts.

Rnd 21: K2tog around. (5 sts)

Cut yarn and using tapestry needle, thread through rem sts to close foot.

EAR (MAKE 2.)

Using circular needle and E, CO 6 sts and join for working in the rnd using Magic Loop method, making sure not to twist sts. PM to indicate beg of rnd.

Rnd 1: Knit all sts.

Rnd 2: (K1f&b, K2) twice. (8 sts)

Rnd 3: (K3, K1f&b) twice. (10 sts)

Rnds 4–8: Knit all sts.

Rnd 9: (Ssk, K1, K2tog) twice. (6 sts)

Rnd 10: Knit all sts.

Cut yarn and using tapestry needle, thread through rem sts to close ear.

FINISHING

Make up the 5 monsters referring to "Monster-Making University" on page 15 for detailed finishing directions. Using monofilament, attach fishing swivel to top of mobile hanger. Whipstitch spokes evenly to bottom of ball on hanger, making sure to alternate colors around so that 2 B spokes are not next to each other. Wrapping ring cover around inside circle of embroidery hoop, st cover onto hoop by whipstitching the 2 sides and ends of cover to each other. Whipstitch 1 spoke to top edge of ring cover. For extra strength, run yarn you use to attach spoke under ring cover and down around ring. Measuring about 8½" over, attach next spoke, repeating until all 5 spokes are attached to cover.

Using spokes as a guide, attach each swing under each spoke by whipstitching both ends to ring cover. Once swings are all attached, determine center between 2 swings and whipstitch dangle to ring cover. Using center dangle, determine center between dangle and swing and st on another dangle, repeating on both sides of center dangle. Be sure to use one dangle in each color between swings! Rep these steps until all dangles are attached.

Using straight pins, place monsters on swings. Before sewing them down, be sure to test hang the mobile to see that monsters on swings are balanced and that mobile does not dip down on one side. Adjust monsters as necessary, and once you're happy and balanced (or at least your mobile is), beg to attach monsters to swings. To do so, whipstitch legs and arms to swing, hiding stitching as much as possible.

Hang your mobile and watch the faces light up on all the kiddos in your life!

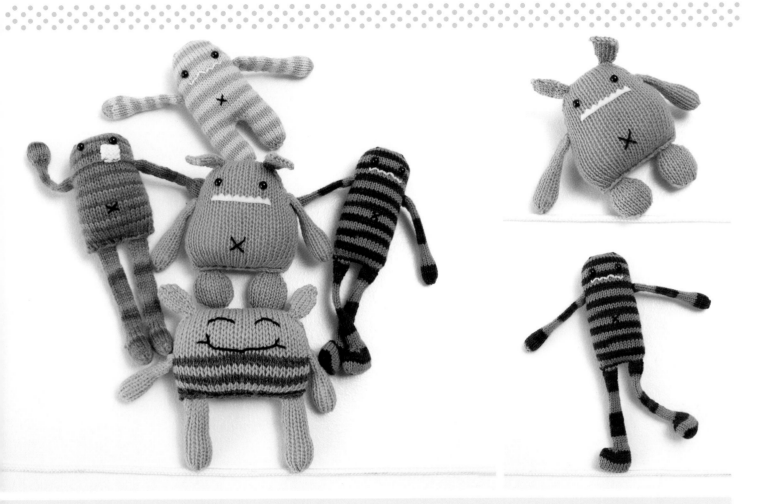

Off the Monster Mobile and Into Your Heart!

These mini monsters are perfectly sized to fit in small hands (and mouths), and are easily packed to take along on all of your monster adventures.

They're also the perfect size to fit into the pocket of the "Monster Pocket Sweater" (page 26) or to swap out with the Monster Friend in the "Pocket Blankie" (page 48). Knit them in whatever yarn you pick for those projects for a fun matched set!

Although the monsters shown were knit in sock yarn on small needles, they can be knit with any yarn and needles. Keep them tiny with sport or DK-weight yarns, or make them bigger with bulky or super bulky-weight yarn. The choice is yours!

Monster SWINGS

Want to make your monsters even snazzier? How about sitting them in swings and hanging them from the ceiling? That's what I do. Though I've designed monsters specifically to sit in these swings, you can use any of my monster patterns. Just knit them with sock yarn on small needles, sew them in the swing, and let them go! These swings look great hanging from any-where: the ceiling, curtain tiebacks, doorknobs, shelves. Have fun!

Skill Level: Intermediate

Finished Size:

- Small Swing: 27" from top of hanger to monster toes
- Medium Swing: 30" from top of hanger to monster toes
- Large Swing: 33" from top of hanger to monster toes

MATERIALS (TO MAKE ALL 3 MONSTERS AND SWINGS)

A 1 skein of Fine from Spud & Chloë (80% wool, 20% silk; 65 g; 248 yds/227 m) in color 7805 Anemone (1)

B 1 skein of Fine from Spud & Chloë in color 7806 Calypso

C 1 skein of Fine from Spud & Chloë in color 7801 Glow Worm

D 1 skein of Fine from Spud & Chloë in color 7812 Lizard

E 1 skein of Fine from Spud & Chloë in color 7823 Hippo

U.S. size 1 (2.25 mm) 40" circular needle (for Magic Loop method), or size needed to obtain gauge

Set of U.S. size 2 (2.75 mm) double-pointed needles

Wooden or plastic embroidery hoops in 7", 8", and 10" diameters (you'll only use the inside ring)

1 pair of 12 mm black safety eyes

2 pairs of 9 mm black safety eyes

Notions: Stuffing, white felt for teeth, fabric glue, row counter (optional), stitch marker, tapestry needle, straight pins (for assembly)

GAUGE

32 sts and 44 rows = 4" in St st on U.S. size 1 (2.25 mm) needle

LARGE SWING (FOR THE 10" HOOP)

RING COVER

Using dpns and 2 strands of E held tog, CO 10 sts into 1 dpn. *Do not join.*

Working in St st, alternate 4 rows E and 4 rows C until piece measures 32", ending on a C stripe.

Loosely BO all sts.

HANGER

Using dpns, waste yarn, and 2 strands of E held tog, use provisional CO (page 9) to CO 4 sts onto 1 dpn.

Knit sts as an I-cord (page 56) for 4".

Making a loop with your I-cord, transfer the 4 provisional CO sts onto needle. Knit across all 8 sts.

Cont as an I-cord, K2tog all sts of next row. (4 sts)

Cont I-cord until it measures 5" from top of loop (or length desired for your swing).

Close-up of large 10" swing hanger.

Ball 1: Switch to C and beg ball, working in the round instead of an I-cord.

Rnd 1: K1f&b all sts, dividing sts to 3 needles as you go. (8 sts)

Rnd 2: K1f&b all sts. (16 sts)

Rnds 3–9: Knit all sts.

Rnd 10: K2tog around. (8 sts)

Stuff ball now.

Rnd 11: Switch back to E, K2tog around. (4 sts)

Sl sts back to 1 dpn and work as an I-cord for 1".

Ball 2: Switch to B, working in the round instead of an I-cord.

Rnd 1: K1f&b all sts, dividing sts to 3 needles as you go. (8 sts)

Rnd 2: K1f&b all sts. (16 sts)

Rnd 3: (K1f&b, K1) around. (24 sts)

Rnds 4–12: Knit all sts.

Rnd 13: (K2tog, K1) around. (16 sts)

Rnd 14: K2tog around. (8 sts)

Stop and stuff now.

Rnd 15: Switch back to E, K2tog around. (4 sts)

Sl sts back to 1 dpn and work as an I-cord for 1".

Ball 3: Switch to D, working in the round instead of an I-cord.

Rnd 1: K1f&b all sts, dividing sts to 3 needles as you go. (8 sts)

Rnd 2: K1f&b all sts. (16 sts)

Rnd 3: K1f&b all sts. (32 sts)

Rnds 4–14: Knit all sts.

Rnd 15: K2tog around. (16 sts)

Rnd 16: K2tog around. (8 sts)

Stuff ball now.

Rnd 17: Switch back to E, K2tog around. (4 sts)

Sl sts back to 1 dpn and work as an I-cord for 1".

Cut yarn and using tapestry needle, thread through rem sts to finish hanger.

ROSCOE, THE STRIPY-SHORTS MONSTER

Use 1 strand each of D, B, and C on U.S. size 1 (2.25 mm) needle to knit the stripy-shorts monster for the large swing.

Leg (Make 2.)

Using dpns and D, evenly CO 5 sts and join, making sure not to twist sts. PM to indicate beg of rnd and beg leg.

Rnd 1: K1f&b in all sts. (10 sts)

Rnd 2: K1f&b in all sts. (20 sts)

Rnds 3–36: Knit all sts.

Rnds 37–54: Knit all sts, alternating 3 rnds B and 3 rnds C. At end of rnd 54, use backward-loop CO (page 13) to CO 6 sts and cut yarn. (26 sts)

Following directions in "Legs to Body" on page 15, transfer leg sts to circular needle as follows. For first leg, put 10 sts on front needle and 16 sts (10 leg sts plus 6 CO sts) on back needle. For second leg, again make sure to cut your yarn and put 16 sts (10 leg sts plus 6 CO sts) on front needle and 10 sts on back needle. You'll have 52 sts total and a new beg of the rnd in middle of Roscoe's second leg.

Body

PM to indicate beg of rnd and using Magic Loop method (page 7) attach yarn and beg body.

Rnds 1–21: Beg with B, knit all sts, alternating 3 rnds B and 3 rnds C.

Rnds 22–60: Switch to D and knit all sts.

Rnd 61: (K2tog, K24) twice. (50 sts)

Rnd 62: Knit all sts.

Rnd 63: (K23, K2tog) twice. (48 sts)

Rnd 64: Knit all sts.

Rnd 65: (K2tog, K22) twice. (46 sts)

Rnd 66: Knit all sts.

Rnd 67: (K21, K2tog) twice. (44 sts)

Rnd 68: Knit all sts.

Rnd 69: (K2tog, K20) twice. (42 sts)

Rnd 70: Knit all sts.

Rnd 71: (K19, K2tog) twice. (40 sts)

Rnd 72: (Ssk, K16, K2tog) twice. (36 sts)

Rnd 73: (Ssk, K14, K2tog) twice. (32 sts)

Rnd 74: (Ssk, K12, K2tog) twice. (28 sts)

Rnd 75: (Ssk, K10, K2tog) twice. (24 sts)

Turn monster body inside out through hole created when casting on additional sts between legs, and work 3-needle BO on rem sts. Turn monster body RS out and keep knitting!

Arm (Make 2.)

Using circular needle and A, CO 14 sts and join for working in the rnd using Magic Loop method, making sure not to twist sts. PM to indicate beg of rnd.

Rnds 1–47: Knit all sts.

Rnd 48: K2tog around. (7 sts)

Cut yarn and using tapestry needle, thread through rem sts to close hand.

Roscoe, the Stripy-Shorts Monster in the large 10" swing.

Smaller Blue-and-Gray-Shorts Roscoe

Finished size: 15" tall

A 1 skein of Comfort DK from Berroco (50% super fine nylon, 50% super fine acrylic; 50 g/1.75 oz; 178 yds/165m) in color 2721 Sprig 3

B 1 skein of Comfort DK from Berroco in color 2713 Dusk

C 1 skein of Comfort DK from Berroco in color 2753 Agean Sea

U.S. size 3 (3.25 mm) needles
12 mm black safety eyes

Larger Black-and-White-Shorts Roscoe

Finished size: 16" tall

A 1 skein of Vintage from Berroco (50% acrylic, 40% wool, 10% nylon; 100 g/3.5 oz; 217 yds/200 m) in color 5125 Aquae 4

B 1 skein of Vintage from Berroco in color 5145 Cast Iron

C 1 skein of Vintage from Berroco in color 5101 Mochi

U.S. size 6 (4 mm) needles

12 mm black safety eyes

Roscoe, out of his swing and into your heart!

These monsters aren't just for swings! Knit Roscoe in your choice of yarn, needles, and color schemes for a wide variety of fun monster toys.

MEDIUM SWING (FOR THE 8" HOOP)

RING COVER

Using dpns and 2 strands of B held tog, CO 8 sts onto 1 dpn. *Do not join.*

Working in St st, alternate 4 rows B and 2 rows D until piece measures 25", ending on a D stripe.

Loosely BO all sts.

HANGER

Using dpns, and 2 strands of B held tog, with provisional CO, CO 4 sts onto 1 dpn.

Knit sts as an I-cord (page 56) for 5".

Making a loop with your I-cord, transfer the 4 provisional CO sts onto needle. Knit across all 8 sts.

Cont as an I-cord, K2tog all sts of next row. (4 sts)

Cont I-cord until it measures 5" from top of loop (or length desired for your swing).

Ball 1: Switch to 2 strands of C and beg ball, working in the round instead of an I-cord.

Rnd 1: K1f&b all sts, dividing sts to 3 needles as you go. (8 sts)

Rnd 2: K1f&b all sts. (16 sts)

Rnd 3: (K1f&b, K1) around. (24 sts)

Rnds 4–12: Knit all sts.

Rnd 13: (K2tog, K1) around. (16 sts)

Rnd 14: K2tog around. (8 sts)

Stuff ball now.

Rnd 15: Switch back to B, K2tog around. (4 sts)

Sl sts back to 1 dpn and work as an I-cord for 1".

Ball 2: Switch to 2 strands of D, working in the round instead of an I-cord.

Rnd 1: K1f&b all sts, dividing sts to 3 needles as you go. (8 sts)

Rnd 2: K1f&b all sts. (16 sts)

Rnds 3–9: Knit all sts.

Rnd 10: K2tog around. (8 sts)

Stuff ball now.

Rnd 11: Switch back to B, K2tog around. (4 sts)

Sl sts back to 1 dpn and work as an I-cord for 1".

Ball 3: Switch to C, working in the round instead of an I-cord.

Rnd 1: K1f&b all sts, dividing sts to 3 needles as you go. (8 sts)

Rnd 2: K1f&b all sts. (16 sts)

Rnd 3: (K1f&b, K1) around. (24 sts)

Rnds 4–12: Knit all sts.

Rnd 13: (K2tog, K1) around. (16 sts)

Rnd 14: K2tog around. (8 sts)

Stuff ball now.

Rnd 15: Switch back to B, K2tog around. (4 sts)

Sl sts back to 1 dpn and work as an I-cord for 1".

Cut yarn and using tapestry needle, thread through rem sts to finish hanger.

VINNY V, THE SMALL-EARS MONSTER

Use 1 strand each of D, C, and B on U.S. size 1 (2.25 mm) needle to knit the small-ears monster for the medium swing.

Body

Using circular needle and D, CO 68 sts and join for working in the rnd using Magic Loop method, making sure not to twist sts. PM to indicate beg of rnd.

Work body in stripes, alternating 3 rnds D and 3 rnds C.

Rnds 1–45: Knit all sts.

Rnd 46: Cont in established stripe patt, (K2tog, K32) twice. (66 sts)

Rnd 47: Knit all sts.

Rnd 48: (K31, K2tog) twice. (64 sts)

Vinny V, the Small-Ears Monster in the medium 8" swing.

Rnd 49: Knit all sts.

Rnd 50: (K2tog, K30) twice. (62 sts)

Rnd 51: Knit all sts.

Rnd 52: (K29, K2tog) twice. (60 sts)

Rnd 53: Knit all sts.

Rnd 54: (K2tog, K28) twice. (58 sts)

Rnd 55: Knit all sts.

Rnd 56: (K27, K2tog) twice. (56 sts)

Rnd 57: Knit all sts.

Rnd 58: (K2tog, K26) twice. (54 sts)

Rnd 59: Knit all sts.

Rnd 60: (K25, K2tog) twice. (52 sts)

Rnd 61: Knit all sts.

Rnd 62: (K2tog, K24) twice. (50 sts)

Rnd 63: Knit all sts.

Rnd 64: (K23, K2tog) twice. (48 sts)

Rnd 65: Knit all sts.

Rnd 66: (K2tog, K22) twice. (46 sts)

Rnd 67: Knit all sts.

Rnd 68: (K21, K2tog) twice. (44 sts)

Rnd 69: Knit all sts.

Rnd 70: (K2tog, K20) twice. (42 sts)

Rnd 71: Knit all sts.

Rnd 72: (K19, K2tog) twice. (40 sts)

Rnd 73: (Ssk, K16, K2tog) twice. (36 sts)

Rnd 74: (Ssk, K14, K2tog) twice. (32 sts)

Rnd 75: (Ssk, K12, K2tog) twice. (28 sts)

Rnd 76: Cont in A, (ssk, K10, K2tog) twice. (24 sts)

Turn monster body inside out, divide sts evenly on the 2 needle tips, and work 3-needle BO on all sts. Turn monster body RS out.

Arm (Make 2.)

Using circular needle and D, CO 12 sts and join for working in the rnd using Magic Loop method, making sure not to twist sts. PM to indicate beg of rnd.

Work arm in stripes, alternating 2 rnds D and 2 rnds C.

Rnds 1–50: Knit all sts.

Rnd 51: With A, K2tog around. (6 sts)

Cut yarn and using tapestry needle, thread through rem sts to close hand.

Leg 1

Using circular needle and D, CO 16 sts and join for working in the rnd using Magic Loop method, making sure not to twist sts. PM to indicate beg of rnd.

Work leg in stripes, alternating 2 rnds D and 2 rnds C.

Rnds 1–60: Knit all sts. At end of rnd 60, *TURN.*

Working just last 8 sts of rnd and cont in established stripe patt (starting with D):

Row 1: Sl 1, purl to end.

Row 2: Sl 1, knit to end.

Work rows 1 and 2 for 9 rows, ending on a purl row.

Rnd 1 of foot: Cont in D, turn once again. PM, this will become new beg of the rnd. Knit across heel sts once more. Using same needle tip, PU 6 sts from left-hand side of heel flap. Flip to other needle tip and knit across held instep sts and PU 6 sts from right-hand side of heel flap. (28 sts)

Rnd 2: Cont in D, K8, K2tog twice, K12, K2tog twice. (24 sts)

Rnd 3: Switch to C (you'll need to cut it from last row worked of the heel and join it back in now). Knit all sts.

Rnd 4: Cont in established stripe patt, K8, K2tog, K12, K2tog. (22 sts)

Rnds 5–18: Knit all sts in established stripe patt.

Rnd 19: With A, K2tog around. (11 sts)

Stuff foot. Cut yarn and using tapestry needle, thread through rem sts to close foot.

Leg 2

Work rnds 1–60 as for leg 1. At end of rnd 60, *DO NOT* turn.

Working just first 8 sts of rnd and cont in established stripe patt (starting with D):

Row 1: Sl 1, knit to end.

Row 2: Sl 1, purl to end.

Work rows 1 and 2 for 10 rows, ending on a purl row.

Cont as for leg 1 with rnd 1 of foot.

Eye Patch

Using circular needle and B, CO 4 sts and join for working in the rnd using Magic Loop method, making sure not to twist sts. PM to indicate beg of rnd.

Rnd 1: K1f&b all sts. (8 sts)

Rnd 2: K1f&b all sts. (16 sts)

Rnd 3: (K1f&b, K1) around. (24 sts)

Rnds 4 and 5: Knit all sts.

Rnd 6: Loosely BO all sts.

Ear (Make 2.)

Using 1 dpn and B, CO 4 sts.

Work as an I-cord.

Rnds 1–3: Knit all sts.

Rnd 4: K1f&b, K3. (5 sts)

Rnds 5–7: Knit all sts.

Rnd 8: K3, K1f&b, K1. (6 sts)

Rnds 9–12: Knit all sts.

Rnd 13: K2tog around. (3 sts)

Cut yarn and using tapestry needle, thread through rem sts to close ear.

Smaller Blue-and-Green Vinny V

Finished size: 16" tall

A 1 skein of Swish DK from Knit Picks (100% superwash merino wool; 50 g; 123 yds) in color Tidepool Heather **(3)**

B 1 skein of Swish DK from Knit Picks in color Big Sky

C 1 skein of Swish DK from Knit Picks in color Parrot

U.S. size 3 (3.25 mm) needles

12 mm black safety eyes

Larger Blue, White, and Yellow Vinny V

Finished size: 19" tall

A 1 skein of Vintage from Berroco (50% acrylic, 40% wool, 10% nylon; 100 g/3.5 oz; 217 yds/200 m) in color 5129 Emerald **(4)**

B 1 skein of Vintage from Berroco in color 5101 Mochi

C 1 skein of Vintage from Berroco in color 5121 Sunny

U.S. size 6 (4 mm) needles

12 mm black safety eyes

How about another Vinny V?

How can a monster named "Vinny V" just live in a swing? Here are two more samples knit in different yarn weights to give you an idea of all the Vinnys waiting to be knit!

SMALL SWING
(FOR THE 7" HOOP)

RING COVER

Using dpns and 2 strands of B held tog, CO 8 sts onto 1 dpn. *Do not join.*

Working in St st, alternate 2 rows B and 2 rows A until piece measures 22", ending on an A stripe.

Loosely BO all sts.

HANGER

Using dpns, waste yarn, 2 strands of A held tog, and provisional CO (page 9), CO 4 sts onto 1 dpn.

Knit sts as an I-cord (page 56) for 4".

Making a loop with your I-cord, transfer the 4 provisional CO sts onto needle. Knit across all 8 sts.

Cont as an I-cord, K2tog all sts of next row. (4 sts)

Cont I-cord until it measures 5" from top of loop (or length desired for your swing).

Ball: Switch to 2 strands of B and beg ball, working in the round instead of an I-cord.

Rnd 1: K1f&b all sts, dividing sts to 3 needles as you go. (8 sts)

Rnd 2: K1f&b all sts. (16 sts)

Rnds 3–9: Knit all sts.

Rnd 10: K2tog around. (8 sts)

Stuff ball now.

Rnd 11: Switch back to A, K2tog around. (4 sts)

Sl sts back to 1 dpn and work as an I-cord for 1".

Rep above directions for ball and 1" I-cord 2 more times so you have 3 balls and your hanger ends in a 1" I-cord.

Cut yarn and using tapestry needle, thread through rem sts to finish hanger.

FRANKIE, THE STRIPY-SWEATER MONSTER

Use 1 strand each of A, B, C, and E on U.S. size 1 (2.25 mm) needle to knit the stripy-sweater monster for the small swing.

Body

Using circular needle and A, CO 40 sts and join for working in the rnd using Magic Loop method, making sure not to twist sts. PM to indicate beg of rnd.

Work body in stripes through rnd 46, alternating 2 rnds B and 2 rnds C.

Rnds 1–36: Knit all sts.

Rnd 37: (K2tog, K16, K2tog) twice. (36 sts)

Frankie, the Stripy-Sweater Monster in the small 7" swing.

Frankie, better in multiples!

Frankie looks great on his swinging perch—or paired up with a fraternal twin, sitting on a bookshelf. Here are two options to get you started if you want to have more than one Frankie (which I know you will).

Smaller Black-and-White-Sweater Frankie

Finished size: 15" tall

A 1 skein of Simplicity from HiKoo (55% merino superwash, 28% acrylic, 17% nylon; 50 g; 107 m) in color 006 Citronella (3)

B 1 skein of Simplicity from HiKoo in color 002 Black

C 1 skein of Simplicity from HiKoo in color 001 White

D 1 skein of Simplicity from HiKoo in color 037 Gun Metal Grey

U.S. size 2 (2.75 mm) needles

9 mm black safety eyes

Larger Blue-and-White-Sweater Frankie

Finished size: 17" tall

A 1 skein of Sweater from Spud & Chloe (55% wool, 45% organic cotton; 100 g; 160 yds/146 m) in color 7502 Grass (4)

B 1 skein of Sweater from Spud & Chloe in color 7510 Splash

C 1 skein of Sweater from Spud & Chloe in color 7500 Ice Cream

D 1 skein of Sweater from Spud & Chloe in color 7507 Moonlight

U.S. size 6 (4 mm) needles

9 mm black safety eyes

Rnd 38: Knit all sts.

Rnd 39: (Ssk, K14, K2tog) twice. (32 sts)

Rnd 40: Knit all sts.

Rnd 41: (Ssk, K12, K2tog) twice. (28 sts)

Rnd 42: Knit all sts.

Rnd 43: (Ssk, K10, K2tog) twice. (24 sts)

Rnd 44: Knit all sts.

Rnd 45: (K2tog) around. (12 sts)

Rnd 46: Knit all sts.

Rnd 47: Switch to A and knit all sts.

Rnd 48: K1f&b all sts. (24 sts)

Rnd 49: (K1f&b, K1) around. (36 sts)

Rnds 50–65: Knit all sts.

Rnd 66: (K2tog) around. (18 sts)

Stuff head and if using safety eyes, add them now.

Rnd 67: (K2tog) around. (9 sts)

Cut yarn and using tapestry needle, thread through rem sts to close head.

Arm (Make 2.)

Using circular needle and A, CO 10 sts and join for working in the rnd using Magic Loop method, making sure not to twist sts. PM to indicate beg of rnd.

Rnds 1–44: Knit all sts, alternating 2 rnds A and 2 rnds C.

Rnd 45: Switch to B and knit all sts. Cont with A for rest of hand.

Rnd 46: (K1f&b, K1f&b, K1, K1f&b, K1f&b) twice. (18 sts)

Rnds 47–55: Knit all sts.

Rnd 56: (K2tog) around. (9 sts)

Stuff hand. Cut yarn and using tapestry needle, thread through rem sts to close hand.

Leg (Make 2.)

Using circular needle and E, CO 12 sts and join for working in the rnd using Magic Loop method, making sure not to twist sts. PM to indicate beg of rnd.

Rnds 1–50: Knit all sts. At end of rnd 50, turn and switch to A.

Working just last 6 sts of rnd:

Row 1: Sl 1, purl to end.

Row 2: Sl 1, knit to end.

Work rows 1 and 2 for 7 rows, ending on a purl row.

Rnd 1 of foot: Turn once more. PM, this will become new beg of the rnd. Knit across heel sts once more. Using same needle tip, PU 3 sts from left-hand side of heel flap. Flip to other needle tip and knit across held instep sts and PU 3 sts from right-hand side of heel flap. (18 sts)

Rnd 2: K6, K2tog, K8, K2tog. (16 sts)

Rnds 3–15: Knit all sts.

Rnd 16: (K2tog) around. (8 sts)

Stuff foot now. Cut yarn and using tapestry needle, thread through rem sts to close foot.

Ear (Make 2.)

Using circular needle and B, CO 6 sts and join for working in the rnd using Magic Loop method, making sure not to twist sts. PM to indicate beg of rnd.

Rnd 1: (K1f&b, K2) twice. (8 sts)

Rnds 2 and 3: Knit all sts.

Rnd 4: (K1f&b, K1) around. (12 sts)

Rnds 5 and 6: Knit all sts.

Rnd 7: (K1f&b, K2) around. (16 sts)

Rnds 8–15: Knit all sts.

Rnd 16: (Ssk, K4, K2tog) twice. (12 sts)

Rnd 17: Knit all sts.

Rnd 18: (Ssk, K2, K2tog) twice. (8 sts)

Rnd 19: Knit all sts.

Rnd 20: K2tog around. (4 sts)

Cut yarn and using tapestry needle, thread through rem sts to close ear.

FINISHING

Make up the 3 monsters referring to "Monster-Making University" on page 15 for detailed finishing directions. Wrapping ring covers around inside circle of their coordinating embroidery hoops, stitch covers onto hoops by whipstitching the 2 sides and ends of the cover to each other. Whipstitch hanger to each swing. For extra strength, run yarn you use to attach hanger under ring cover and down around ring.

Using straight pins, place monsters on swings. Before sewing them down, be sure to test hang each one to see that monsters on swings are balanced and centered. Adjust monsters as necessary, and once you're happy with how everything looks, whipstitch each monster to its swing, hiding your stitching as much as possible. Hang your swings!

Monster Safety

I've included safety eyes and felt teeth to make the monsters shown exactly as I made them. If you want to be able to have munchkins play with your monsters, you might consider embroidering the faces to make them baby safe.

Monster BOOKENDS

Boy, how we do love kids' books in my house! Which means we need lots of bookends. These are great for holding up books, or as paperweights, or for just decorating. After knitting these samples, I found myself obsessed and thinking of reasons to put them everywhere. They're a great, simple, quick knit, making them perfect shower gifts. How cute would it be for the new mama to open a box with a couple of these and several of your favorite baby books?

Skill Level: Intermediate

Finished Size: Approx 7" tall and 5" across at widest point

MATERIALS (TO MAKE ALL 4 BOOKENDS)

A 1 skein of Swish DK from Knit Picks (100% superwash merino wool; 50 g; 123 yds) in color Big Sky (3)

B 1 skein of Swish DK from Knit Picks in color Tidepool Heather

C 1 skein of Swish DK from Knit Picks in color Cobblestone Heather

D 1 skein of Swish DK from Knit Picks in color Parrot

E 1 skein of Swish DK from Knit Picks in color Coal

F 1 skein of Swish DK from Knit Picks in color White

Scrap of black yarn for eyes in same weight and fiber as project yarn

Scrap of white yarn for tooth in same weight and fiber as project yarn

U.S. size 5 (3.75 mm) 40" circular needle (for Magic Loop method), or size needed to obtain gauge

1 additional needle, straight, circular, or double pointed, in same size as circular needle (for 3-needle BO)

15 mm black safety eyes

Notions: White felt for teeth, fabric glue, stuffing, rice or PVC "beans" to weight the base, 4 sandwich-sized plastic ziplock bags, row counter (optional), stitch marker, tapestry needle, straight pins (to help with assembly)

GAUGE

22 sts and 32 rows = 4" in St st

EYE-PATCH MONSTER

Using circular needle and A, CO 70 sts and join for working in the rnd using Magic Loop method (page 7), making sure not to twist sts. PM to indicate beg of rnd.

Rnds 1–20: Knit all sts.

Rnd 21: (K2tog, K33) twice. (68 sts)

Rnd 22: Knit all sts.

Rnd 23: (K32, K2tog) twice. (66 sts)

Rnd 24: Knit all sts.

Rnd 25: (K2tog, K31) twice. (64 sts)

Rnd 26: Knit all sts.

Rnd 27: (K30, K2tog) twice. (62 sts)

Rnd 28: Knit all sts.

Rnd 29: (K2tog, K29) twice. (60 sts)

Rnd 30: Knit all sts.

Rnd 31: (K28, K2tog) twice. (58 sts)

Rnd 32: Knit all sts.

Rnd 33: (K2tog, K27) twice. (56 sts)

Rnd 34: Knit all sts.

Rnd 35: (K26, K2tog) twice. (54 sts)

Rnd 36: Knit all sts.

Rnd 37: (K2tog, K25) twice. (52 sts)

Rnd 38: Knit all sts.

Rnd 39: (K24, K2tog) twice. (50 sts)

Rnd 40: (Ssk, K21, K2tog) twice. (46 sts)

Rnd 41: (Ssk, K19, K2tog) twice. (42 sts)

Rnd 42: (Ssk, K17, K2tog) twice. (38 sts)

Rnd 43: (Ssk, K15, K2tog) twice. (34 sts)

Rnd 44: (Ssk, K13, K2tog) twice. (30 sts)

Turn body inside out, divide sts evenly on the 2 needle tips, and work 3-needle BO on all sts. Turn body RS out.

EAR (MAKE 2.)

Using circular needle and B, CO 10 sts and join for working in the rnd using Magic Loop method, making sure not to twist sts. PM to indicate beg of rnd.

Rnd 1: Knit all sts.

Rnd 2: (K1f&b, K3, K1f&b) twice. (14 sts)

Eye-Patch Monster

Rnd 3: Knit all sts.

Rnd 4: (K1f&b, K5, K1f&b) twice. (18 sts)

Rnds 5–15: Knit all sts.

Rnd 16: (Ssk, K5, K2tog) twice. (14 sts)

Rnd 17: Knit all sts.

Rnd 18: (Ssk, K3, K2tog) twice. (10 sts)

Rnd 19: K2tog around. (5 sts)

Cut yarn and using tapestry needle, thread through rem sts to close ear.

EYE PATCH

Using circular needle and B, CO 6 sts and join for working in the rnd using Magic Loop method, making sure not to twist sts. PM to indicate beg of rnd.

Rnd 1: K1f&b around. (12 sts)

Rnd 2: (K1f&b, K1) around. (18 sts)

Rnd 3: (K1f&b, K2) around. (24 sts)

Rnd 4: (K1f&b, K3) around. (30 sts)

Rnds 5 and 6: Knit all sts.

Rnd 7: BO all sts.

Toothy Monster

TOOTHY MONSTER

Work body in stripe patt alternating 3 rnds C and 3 rnds D.

Using circular needle and C, CO 70 sts and join for working in the rnd using Magic Loop method, making sure not to twist sts. PM to indicate beg of rnd.

Rnds 1–17: Knit all sts.

Rnd 18: BO first 35 sts of rnd, knit to end. (35 sts)

Rnd 19: PU first 35 sts of rnd through back loop only, knit to end. (70 sts) *These 2 rnds will make a ridge that creates the mouth.*

Rnd 20: Knit all sts.

Rnd 21: (K2tog, K33) twice. (68 sts)

Rnd 22: Knit all sts.

Rnd 23: (K32, K2tog) twice. (66 sts)

Rnd 24: Knit all sts.

Rnd 25: (K2tog, K31) twice. (64 sts)

Rnd 26: Knit all sts.

Rnd 27: (K30, K2tog) twice. (62 sts)

Rnd 28: Knit all sts.

Rnd 29: (K2tog, K29) twice. (60 sts)

Rnd 30: Knit all sts.

Rnd 31: (K28, K2tog) twice. (58 sts)

Rnd 32: Knit all sts.

Rnd 33: (K2tog, K27) twice. (56 sts)

Rnd 34: Knit all sts.

Rnd 35: (K26, K2tog) twice. (54 sts)

Rnd 36: Knit all sts.

Rnd 37: (K2tog, K25) twice. (52 sts)

Rnd 38: Knit all sts.

Rnd 39: (K24, K2tog) twice. (50 sts)

Rnd 40: (Ssk, K21, K2tog) twice. (46 sts)

Rnd 41: (Ssk, K19, K2tog) twice. (42 sts)

Rnd 42: (Ssk, K17, K2tog) twice. (38 sts)

Rnd 43: (Ssk, K15, K2tog) twice. (34 sts)

Rnd 44: (Ssk, K13, K2tog) twice. (30 sts)

Turn monster inside out, divide sts evenly on the 2 needle tips, and work 3-needle BO on all sts. Turn monster RS out.

EAR (MAKE 2.)

Using circular needle and D, CO 10 sts and join for working in the rnd using Magic Loop method, making sure not to twist sts. PM to indicate beg of rnd.

Rnd 1: Knit all sts.

Rnd 2: (K1f&b, K3, K1f&b) twice. (14 sts)

Rnd 3: Knit all sts.

Rnd 4: (K1f&b, K5, K1f&b) twice. (18 sts)

Rnd 5: Knit all sts.

Rnd 6: (K1f&b, K7, K1f&b) twice. (22 sts)

Rnds 7–14: Knit all sts.

Divide sts evenly on the 2 needle tips and work 3-needle BO on all sts.

TOOTH

With head facing upside down, count from edge to 16th st of mouth. Using F, beg in 16th st, PU 6 sts in 16th through 11th sts.

Knit 10 rows (garter st).

BO all sts.

BASE FOR BOTH MONSTERS

Attach eye patch and safety eyes before starting the base.

Using circular needle and B, PU 70 sts from CO edge of body, join and work in the round using Magic Loop method.

Rnds 1–4: Knit all sts.

Rnd 5: (K2tog, K5) around. (60 sts)

Rnd 6: (K2tog, K4) around. (50 sts)

Rnd 7: (K2tog, K3) around. (40 sts)

Rnd 8: K2tog around. (20 sts)

Stuff body, leaving bottom 25% or so unstuffed. If you choose to use safety eyes, add them now. Fill plastic ziplock bag with rice or "beans" and add it below stuffing. I used approx 1½ cups of rice for each bookend.

Rnd 9: K2tog around. (10 sts)

Cut yarn and using tapestry needle, thread through rem sts to close base.

FINISHING

Weave in all ends. Play around with ear placement and whipstitch ears on top of head. Add the face now, checking out "Monster-Making University" on page 15.

Grab some books and prop 'em up with your new monster buddy!

Make It Your Monster!

I decided to play around with colors and stripes on these guys and switch things up, adding stripes to one of the plain monster bodies, and using a single color on a toothy-monster body. To make the black-and-white sample shown, use the stripes from the toothy-monster body, substituting E for A and F for B on a plain monster body. To make the darker blue-and-green monster, knit a toothy-monster body all in B, and use D for the ears. I encourage you to use your imagination and go wild with colors!

Monster
PILLOWS

Who doesn't love to snuggle with a monster? I knew as soon as I started on my monster nursery that it would need to have lots of pillows. These came out so snuggly and cuddly, I love them! My kiddo loves them too; they were great to prop him up on for tummy time, and when he began crawling they were a fun and colorful target for him to move toward. Plus, if you're feeling down, there's nothing that will cheer you up faster than a big monster hug!

Skill Level: Intermediate

Finished Size (excluding limbs):

- Small: 12" x 16"
- Medium: 14" x 14"
- Large: 16" x 16"

MATERIALS (TO MAKE ALL 3 PILLOWS)

A 1 skein of SimpliWorsted from HiKoo (55% superwash merino, 28% acrylic, 17% nylon; 100 g; 140 yds) in color 010 Deep Turquoise (5)

B 1 skein of SimpliWorsted from HiKoo in color 007 Kiwi

C 1 skein of SimpliWorsted from HiKoo in color 027 Nile Blue

D 1 skein of SimpliWorsted from HiKoo in color 037 Gun Metal Grey

E 1 skein of SimpliWorsted from HiKoo in color 009 Aqua Mint

U.S. size 8 (5 mm) 16" circular needle for pillows and 40" circular needle (for Magic Loop method) for limbs and ears, or size needed to obtain gauge

12" x 16" pillow form

14" x 14" pillow form

16" x 16" pillow form

Scrap of black yarn for eyes and mouth

Notions: Row counter (optional), stitch marker, tapestry needle, straight pins (to help with assembly)

GAUGE

16 sts and 24 rows = 4" in St st

SMALL GREEN STRIPY PILLOW

Using 16" circular needle and A, CO 128 sts and join, making sure not to twist sts. PM to indicate beg of rnd and beg body.

Alternating 6 rnds A and 6 rnds B, knit until you have 3 A stripes.

Switch to B and knit until piece measures 12" from CO edge.

Turn body inside out, divide sts evenly on the 2 needle tips, and work 3-needle BO on all sts. Turn body RS out.

ARM (MAKE 2.)

Using circular needle and B, CO 18 sts and join for working in the rnd using Magic Loop method (page 7), making sure not to twist sts. PM to indicate beg of rnd.

Rnds 1–40: Knit all sts.

Rnd 41: K2tog around. (9 sts)

Cut yarn and using tapestry needle, thread through rem sts to close hand.

LEG (MAKE 2.)

Using circular needle and B, CO 20 sts and join for working in the rnd using Magic Loop method, making sure not to twist sts. PM to indicate beg of rnd.

Rnds 1–45: Knit all sts.

Rnd 46: K2tog around. (10 sts)

Rnd 47: K2tog around. (5 sts)

Cut yarn and using tapestry needle, thread through rem sts to close foot.

EAR (MAKE 2.)

Using circular needle and B, CO 12 sts and join for working in the rnd using Magic Loop method, making sure not to twist sts. PM to indicate beg of rnd.

Rnd 1: Knit all sts.

Rnd 2: (K1f&b, K5) twice. (14 sts)

Rnd 3: (K6, K1f&b) twice. (16 sts)

Rnd 4: (K1f&b, K7) twice. (18 sts)

Rnd 5: (K8, K1f&b) twice. (20 sts)

Rnds 6–15: Knit all sts.

Rnd 16: (Ssk, K6, K2tog) twice. (16 sts)

Rnd 17: (Ssk, K4, K2tog) twice. (12 sts)

Rnd 18: (Ssk, K2, K2tog) twice. (8 sts)

Rnd 19: K2tog around. (4 sts)

Cut yarn and using tapestry needle, thread through rem sts to close ear.

MEDIUM BLUE-AND-GRAY STRIPY PILLOW

Using circular needle and C, CO 112 sts and join, making sure not to twist sts. PM to indicate beg of rnd and beg body using Magic Loop method.

Alternating 6 rnds C and 6 rnds D, knit until you have 4 C and 3 D stripes.

Switch to E and knit until piece measures 14" from CO edge.

Turn body inside out, divide sts evenly on the 2 needle tips, and work 3-needle BO on all sts. Turn body RS out.

ARM (MAKE 2.)

Using circular needle and D, CO 20 sts and join for working in the rnd using Magic Loop method, making sure not to twist sts. PM to indicate beg of rnd.

Rnds 1–36: Knit all sts.

Rnd 37: Switch to E and knit all sts.

Rnd 38: Cont in E to end, (K1f&b, K8, K1f&b) twice. (24 sts)

Rnds 39–52: Knit all sts.

Rnd 53: K2tog around. (12 sts)

Rnd 54: K2tog around. (6 sts)

Cut yarn and using tapestry needle, thread through rem sts to close hand.

LEG (MAKE 2.)

Using circular needle and C, CO 24 sts and join for working in the rnd using Magic Loop method, making sure not to twist sts. PM to indicate beg of rnd.

Rnds 1–40: Knit all sts.

Rnd 41: Switch to E and knit all sts.

Rnd 42: Cont in E to end, K10, K1f&b in next 4 sts, knit to end. (28 sts)

Rnd 43: K12, K1f&b in next 4 sts, K12. (32 sts)

Rnd 44: K14, K1f&b in next 4 sts, K14. (36 sts)

Rnd 45: K16, K1f&b in next 4 sts, K16. (40 sts)

Rnd 46: K18, K1f&b in next 4 sts, K18. (44 sts)

Rnd 47: K20, K1f&b in next 4 sts, K20. (48 sts)

Rnd 48: K23, K1f&b in next 2 sts, K23. (50 sts)

Rnds 49–59: Knit all sts.

Rnd 60: (K2tog, K21, K2tog) twice. (46 sts)

Cut yarn, leaving long tail, and use tapestry needle and Kitchener st to close foot.

LARGE BLUE EYE-PATCH PILLOW

Using 16" circular needle and A, CO 128 sts and join, making sure not to twist sts. PM to indicate beg of rnd and beg body using Magic Loop method.

Alternating 9 rnds A and 2 rnds E, knit until piece measures 16" from CO edge.

Turn body inside out, divide sts evenly on the 2 needle tips, and work 3-needle BO on all sts. Turn body RS out.

ARM (MAKE 2.)

Using circular needle and A, CO 22 sts and join for working in the rnd using Magic Loop method, making sure not to twist sts. PM to indicate beg of rnd.

Rnds 1–46: Knit all sts.

Rnd 47: K2tog around. (11 sts)

Rnd 48: K2tog around, end K1. (6 sts)

Cut yarn and using tapestry needle, thread through rem sts to close hand.

FOOT (MAKE 2.)

Using circular needle and E, CO 30 sts and join for working in the rnd using Magic Loop method, making sure not to twist sts. PM to indicate beg of rnd.

Rnds 1 and 2: Knit all sts.

Rnd 3: (K1f&b, K13, K1f&b) twice. (34 sts)

Rnd 4: Knit all sts.

Rnd 5: (K1f&b, K15, K1f&b) twice. (38 sts)

Rnd 6: Knit all sts.

Rnd 7: (K1f&b, K17, K1f&b) twice. (42 sts)

Rnd 8: Knit all sts.

Rnd 9: (K1f&b, K19, K1f&b) twice. (46 sts)

Rnd 10: Knit all sts.

Rnd 11: (K1f&b, K21, K1f&b) twice. (50 sts)

Rnds 12–26: Knit all sts.

Rnd 27: (K2tog, K3) around. (40 sts)

Rnd 28: (K2tog, K2) around. (30 sts)

Rnd 29: (K2tog, K1) around. (20 sts)

Rnd 30: K2tog around. (10 sts)

Cut yarn and using tapestry needle, thread through rem sts to close foot.

EYE PATCH

Using circular needle and E, CO 6 sts and join for working in the rnd using Magic Loop method, making sure not to twist sts. PM to indicate beg of rnd.

Rnd 1: K1f&b all sts. (12 sts)

Rnd 2: (K1f&b, K1) around. (18 sts)

Rnd 3: (K1f&b, K2) around. (24 sts)

Rnd 4: (K1f&b, K3) around. (30 sts)

Rnd 5: (K1f&b, K4) around. (36 sts)

Rnd 6: (K1f&b, K5) around. (42 sts)

Rnd 7: (K1f&b, K6) around. (48 sts)

Rnd 8: (K1f&b, K7) around. (54 sts)

Rnd 9: (K1f&b, K8) around. (60 sts)

Rnd 10: Knit all sts.

Rnd 11: Loosely BO all sts.

FINISHING

Stuff all limbs. Weave in all ends. Slip pillow forms into their respective covers. Attach legs to inside of bottom edges using a running stitch, then use a running stitch to close the covers. Add arms, ears, and faces, referring to "Monster-Making University" (page15). Throw your new pillows on a chair!

Monster
Tissue and Wipes
BOX COVERS

I've told Mr. Danger since the day we met that if I start knitting tea cozies, that's it, I've gone over the edge and lost my marbles. So when I started on tissue and wipes box covers, I was a little afraid of what he might do. He was skeptical, but once he saw the finished result, he admitted he loves the dressed-up necessities in our kiddo's room! You have to have wipes, but who says they have to look boring?

Skill Level: Intermediate

Finished Sizes:

- Tissue Box Cover: To fit standard square tissue box, 17" circumference and 5⅛" tall
- Wipes Box Cover: To fit standard wipes box, 25" circumference and 4⅛" tall

These covers are designed to fit snugly so they don't fall off. Make sure your gauge is right on for the best fit.

MATERIALS

For Tissue Box Cover

A 1 skein of Merino Worsted from Shibuiknits (100% superwash merino; 100 g/3.5 oz; 191 yds/175 m) in color 7495 Wasabi (4)

2 black domed buttons, ¾" diameter

For Wipes Box Cover

B 1 skein of Merino Worsted from Shibuiknits in color 3601 Breeze

C 1 skein of Merino Worsted from Shibuiknits in color 1601 Dragonfly

2 black domed buttons, ⅝" diameter

For Both Covers

U.S. size 8 (5 mm) 40" circular needle (for Magic Loop method), or size needed to obtain gauge

U.S. size 5 (3.75 mm) 40" circular needle (for Magic Loop method)

1 additional needle, straight, circular, or double pointed, in same size as larger circular needle (for 3-needle BO)

Scrap of white yarn for teeth

Notions: Row counter (optional), stitch marker, tapestry needle, straight pins (to help with assembly)

GAUGE

18 sts and 22 rows = 4" in St st on U.S. size 8 (5 mm) needle

Elastic BO

Work 2 sts in patt. Where second st is a knit st: *Insert left-hand needle into front of both sts on right-hand needle (on "top" of right-hand needle). Knit the 2 sts tog tbl. Work next st in patt and rep from *.

Where second st is a purl st: *Insert left-hand needle into the back of both sts on right-hand needle ("below" right-hand needle). Purl the 2 sts tog. Work next st in patt and rep from *.

TISSUE BOX COVER

Using larger circular needle and A, CO 20 sts for the top. *Do not join.*

Work in St st until piece measures 2", ending on a WS row.

Next row (RS): K4, BO 12 sts, knit to end. (8 sts)

Next row: P4, turn work, and use knit CO to CO 12 sts. Turn work once again, purl to end. (20 sts)

Work in St st for 2" more, ending on a WS row.

Loosely BO all sts.

ARM (MAKE 2.)

Using larger circular needle and A, CO 10 sts and join for working in the rnd using Magic Loop method, making sure not to twist sts. PM to indicate beg of rnd.

Rnds 1–40: Knit all sts.

Rnd 41: K1f&b all sts. (20 sts)

Rnds 42–52: Knit all sts.

Rnd 53: K2tog around. (10 sts)

Stuff hands now. Cut yarn and using tapestry needle, thread through rem sts to close hand.

LEG (MAKE 2.)

Using larger circular needle and A, CO 16 sts and join for working in the rnd using Magic Loop method, making sure not to twist sts. PM to indicate beg of rnd.

Rnd 1: Knit all sts.

Rnd 2: (K1f&b, K6, K1f&b) twice. (20 sts)

Rnd 3: Knit all sts.

Rnd 4: (K1f&b, K8, K1f&b) twice. (24 sts)

Rnd 5: Knit all sts.

Rnd 6: (K1f&b, K10, K1f&b) twice. (28 sts)

Rnds 7–12: Knit all sts.

Work short rows as follows.

Row 1: K9, ssk, K6, K2tog, sl 1, turn.

Row 2: P2tog, P6, sl 1-P1-psso, sl 1, turn.

Row 3: Ssk, K6, K2tog, sl 1, turn.

Work rows 2 and 3 until 16 sts rem (you'll end on a purl row).

Next row: Ssk, K6, K2tog, K6. (14 sts)

Beg work in rnd again for leg.

Rnd 1: K2tog, knit to last 2 sts, K2tog. (12 sts)

Rnds 2–48: Knit all sts.

Rnd 49: BO all sts.

WIPES BOX COVER

Using larger circular needle and B, CO 20 sts for the base. *Do not join.* Work in St st until piece measures 7½" from CO edge, ending on a WS row.

Loosely BO all sts.

SIDES

Using A, PU 20 sts from each end and 32 sts from each long side. (104 sts)

Divide half of the sts onto each needle tip to work in the round using Magic Loop method.

SIDES

Using circular needle and A, PU 20 sts from each of the 4 sides of the square. Divide half of the sts on each needle tip to work in the round using Magic Loop method (page 7). You'll have 80 sts total.

Work in St st (knit every rnd) until piece measures 5" from picked-up edge.

Next rnd: Switch to smaller needles and K2tog around. (40 sts)

Work 4 rnds in K1, P1 rib. Work elastic BO in patt on all sts. (See note on page 87.)

Work in St st (knit every rnd) until piece measures 4½" from picked-up edge.

Next rnd: K2tog around. (52 sts)

Switch to smaller needles and work 4 rnds in K1, P1 rib.

Work elastic BO in patt all sts. (See note on page 87.)

ARM (MAKE 2.)

Using larger circular needle and B, CO 16 sts and join for working in the rnd using Magic Loop method, making sure not to twist sts. PM to indicate beg of rnd.

Rnds 1–18: Knit all sts.

Rnd 19: K2tog around. (8 sts)

Cut yarn and using tapestry needle, thread through rem sts to close hand.

FOOT (MAKE 2.)

Using larger circular needle and C, CO 14 sts and join for working in the rnd using Magic Loop method, making sure not to twist sts. PM to indicate beg of rnd.

Rnd 1: Knit all sts.

Rnd 2: (K1f&b, K5, K1f&b) twice. (18 sts)

Rnd 3: Knit all sts.

Rnd 4: (K1f&b, K7, K1f&b) twice. (22 sts)

Rnds 5–12: Knit all sts.

Rnd 13: (Ssk, K7, K2tog) twice. (18 sts)

Rnd 14: (Ssk, K5, K1f&b) twice. (14 sts)

Rnd 15: (Ssk, K3, K1f&b) twice. (10 sts)

Turn foot inside out, divide sts evenly on the 2 needle tips, and work 3-needle BO on all sts. Turn foot RS out.

EAR (MAKE 2.)

Using larger circular needle and C, CO 12 sts and join for working in the rnd using Magic Loop method, making sure not to twist sts. PM to indicate beg of rnd.

Rnd 1: Knit all sts.

Rnd 2: (K1f&b, K4, K1f&b) twice. (16 sts)

Rnd 3: Knit all sts.

Rnd 4: (K1f&b, K6, K1f&b) twice. (20 sts)

Rnds 5–11: Knit all sts.

Divide sts evenly on the 2 needle tips and work 3-needle BO on all sts.

EYE PATCH

Using larger circular needle and C, CO 6 sts and join for working in the rnd using Magic Loop method, making sure not to twist sts. PM to indicate beg of rnd.

Rnd 1: K1f&b all sts. (12 sts)

Rnd 2: (K1f&b, K1) around. (18 sts)

Rnd 3: (K1f&b, K2) around. (24 sts)

Rnds 4 and 5: Knit all sts.

Rnd 6: BO all sts.

FINISHING

Weave in all ends. Stuff tissue-box-cover feet and use row-to-row mattress st (page 35) to sew seam on bottom of foot shut. Referring to "Monster-Making University" on page 15, make up your monsters. Sew buttons on for eyes and use the scrap white yarn to embroider the teeth. I guarantee, having these tissue and wipes box covers in your nursery will make diaper changes way more fun!

Monster Safety

I used buttons and embroidered teeth to make these covers wash-able. Buttons should be used with caution around babies! Be sure to check them regularly to be sure little fingers can't get them off and choke on them.

Monster CHAIR

I couldn't help myself, I just had to design a piece of monsterized, knitted furniture for Presley's nursery. This chair is so fun, and it certainly has become a conversation starter in our house! And, knitting furniture is actually really, surprisingly fun. More than anything, though, I love the fact that it's a special spot for my kiddo and me to enjoy story time.

Skill Level: Intermediate

Finished Size: Approx 25" tall when stuffed

MATERIALS

MC 12 skeins of Vintage Chunky from Berroco (50% acrylic, 40% wool, 10% nylon; 100 g/3.5 oz; 130 yds/120 m) in color 6165 Wasabi (5)

CC 3 skeins of Vintage Chunky from Berroco in color 6125 Aquae

U.S. size 17 (12.75 mm) 24" or longer circular needle, or size needed to obtain gauge

1 additional needle, straight, circular, or double pointed in same size as circular needle (for 3-needle BO)

2 body pillows, or 2 queen-size comforters for stuffing

Scraps of white and black yarn for embroidering face

Notions: Row counter (optional), stitch marker, tapestry needle

GAUGE

7 sts and 12 rows = 4" in St st with 3 strands held tog

It can be very difficult to find needles in U.S. size 17 (12.75 mm). I recommend at least a 24" circular needle, but it would probably be easier with a longer circular needle if you can find it.

CHAIR

Chair is worked holding 3 strands of yarn tog throughout.

Using circular needle and 3 strands of MC held tog, CO 90 sts. *Do not join.*

Row 1: Knit all sts.

Row 2: Purl all sts.

Row 3: K1f&b, K42, K1f&b, K2, K1f&b, K42, K1f&b. (94 sts)

Row 4: Purl all sts.

Row 5: K1f&b, K44, K1f&b, K2, K1f&b, K44, K1f&b. (98 sts)

Row 6: Purl all sts.

Row 7: K1f&b, K46, K1f&b, K2, K1f&b, K46, K1f&b. (102 sts)

Rows 8–18: Work in St st in MC.

Rows 19 and 20: Switch to 3 strands of CC held tog and cont to work in St st.

Rows 21–42: Cont in St st using 3 strands of each color, and alternating 8 rows MC and 2 rows CC. You'll end on 2 rows MC.

Shape seat:

Row 1: K28, ssk, K42, K2tog, sl 1, turn.

Row 2: P2tog, P42, sl 1-P1-psso, sl 1, turn.

Row 3: Ssk, K42, K2tog, sl 1, turn.

Rep rows 2 and 3 until you have 78 sts, ending on row 2 (WS).

Next row: Ssk, K7, K2tog, knit to end of row. (76 sts)

Work next 24 rows in St st with 3 strands of MC held tog.

Next row: (K2tog, K2) across. (57 sts)

Purl 1 row.

Next row: (K2tog, K1) across. (38 sts)

Purl 1 row.

Next row: K2tog across. (19 sts)

Next row: P2tog across, end P1. (10 sts)

Cut yarn and using tapestry needle, thread through rem sts to close head.

ARM (MAKE 2.)

Using circular needle and 3 strands of MC held tog, CO 24 sts. *Do not join.*

Work in St st until arm measures 11".

Next row: K2tog across. (12 sts)

Cut yarn and using tapestry needle, thread through rem sts to close arm.

EAR (MAKE 2.)

Using circular needle and 3 strands of CC held tog, CO 18 sts. *Do not join.*

Row 1: Knit all sts.

Rows 2, 4, 6, and 8: Purl all sts.

Row 3: (K1f&b, K7, K1f&b) twice. (22 sts)

Row 5: (K1f&b, K9, K1f&b) twice. (26 sts)

Row 7: (K1f&b, K11, K1f&b) twice. (30 sts)

Row 9: (K1f&b, K13, K1f&b) twice. (34 sts)

Cont in St st until ear measures 7", ending on a RS row.

With WS facing out, divide sts evenly on the 2 needle tips and work 3-needle BO all sts. Turn ear RS out.

FINISHING

Weave in all ends. Using a row-to-row mattress st (page 35), sew up back seam of chair, making sure to leave a bottom opening for stuffing. If using body pillows for stuffing, fold one in half to fill out "head" and back section of chair. Fold second body pillow in half and place it in "seat" part of body to create a general chair shape. If using comforters, stuff one up in head area and one in bottom "seat" area.

Once stuffed, use st-to-st mattress stitch (page 32) to close bottom seam of chair. Stuff arms and ears, and use row-to-row mattress st to close them. Whipstitch ears to top of head and arms to sides of body. Use scrap yarn to embroider eyes and mouth.

Grab a kiddo and a book and plop down in your new awesome chair for story time!

Monster Tip

I know, I know, another pattern not written in the round. I chose to design this pattern knit flat with seams, because finding needles in this size is challenging. I couldn't even find U.S. size 17 (12.75 mm) double-pointed needles anywhere! So, if you're able to find double-pointed needles or a circular needle that seems to accommodate knitting in the round, go for it!

This is my mon-sterized take on an old classic. I think I've seen every variety of stacking toy there is, but none of them were too interesting. I figured I could make something way more creative, and I definitely think this does the trick! Presley loves this thing; he prefers to throw the rings rather than stack them, but hey, whatever makes him happy, right?

Skill Level: Experienced

Finished Size: Approx 21" tall

Largest ring is approx 13" across.

MATERIALS

A 3 skeins of Vintage from Berroco (50% acrylic, 40% wool, 10% nylon; 100 g/3.5 oz; 217 yds/200 m) in color 5107 Cracked Pepper **(4)**

B 2 skeins of Vintage from Berroco in color 5129 Emerald *(You will use approx 20 yds in the second skein; you can choose to do some of the limbs in a different color if you would like to avoid buying a second skein.)*

C 1 skein of Vintage from Berroco in color 5112 Minty

D 1 skein of Vintage from Berroco in color 5175 Fennel

E 1 skein of Vintage from Berroco in color 5125 Aquae

F 1 skein of Vintage from Berroco in color 5121 Sunny

2 U.S. size 6 (4 mm) circular needles, 24" and 40" long, or size needed to obtain gauge

Scrap of black yarn for embroidering eyes

Notions: Stuffing, stitch marker, row counter (optional), tapestry needle

GAUGE

20 sts and 24 rows = 4" in St st

BIGGEST RING

With 40" circular needle, waste yarn, and B, use provisional CO (page 8) to CO 110 sts. *Do not join.*

Knit 1 row. Divide sts in half on each needle tip to work in the round using Magic Loop method (page 7). Join, working from last st knitted to first st knitted.

Knit until piece measures 10" from CO edge. Cut yarn, leaving an extra-long tail.

Referring to "Making Stuffed Rings" on page 11, move provisional CO sts from waste yarn to 24" circular needle. Pull this needle up through center of ring just knitted (make sure RS is outside) and use tapestry needle to work Kitchener st to close ring. The provisional CO makes every other st twisted on the waste yarn, so be sure to untwist sts as you go by knitting into the back of these sts. Cont Kitchener st around all sts, stopping to stuff ring every couple inches. When you've worked all sts and ring is completely stuffed, close any hole that is left. If you end up 1 st short, PU extra st at end.

ARM (MAKE 2.)

Using longer circular needle and B, CO 16 sts and join for working in the rnd using Magic Loop method, making sure not to twist sts. PM to indicate beg of rnd.

Rnds 1–36: Knit all sts.

Rnd 37: K2tog around. (8 sts)

Cut yarn and using tapestry needle, thread through rem sts to close hand.

FOOT (MAKE 2.)

Using longer circular needle and C, CO 24 sts and join for working in the rnd using Magic Loop method, making sure not to twist sts. PM to indicate beg of rnd.

Rnd 1: Knit all sts.

Rnd 2: (K1f&b, K11) twice. (26 sts)

Rnd 3: Knit all sts.

Rnd 4: (K12, K1f&b) twice. (28 sts)

Rnd 5: Knit all sts.

Rnd 6: (K1f&b, K13) twice. (30 sts)

Rnd 7: Knit all sts.

Rnd 8: (K14, K1f&b) twice. (32 sts)

Rnd 9: Knit all sts.

Rnd 10: (K1f&b, K15) twice. (34 sts)

Rnd 11: Knit all sts.

Rnd 12: (K16, K1f&b) twice. (36 sts)

Rnds 13–22: Knit all sts.

Rnd 23: (Ssk, K14, K2tog) twice. (32 sts)

Rnd 24: (Ssk, K12, K2tog) twice. (28 sts)

Rnd 25: (Ssk, K10, K2tog) twice. (24 sts)

Turn foot inside out, divide sts evenly on the 2 needle tips, and work 3-needle BO on all sts. Turn foot RS out.

EAR (MAKE 2.)

Using longer circular needle and C, CO 12 sts and join for working in the rnd using Magic Loop method, making sure not to twist sts. PM to indicate beg of rnd.

Rnd 1: Knit all sts.

Rnd 2: (K1f&b, K5) twice. (14 sts)

Rnd 3: Knit all sts.

Rnd 4: (K6, K1f&b) twice. (16 sts)

Rnds 5–16: Knit all sts.

Rnd 17: K2tog around. (8 sts)

Rnd 18: Knit all sts.

Rnd 19: K2tog around. (4 sts)

Cut yarn and using tapestry needle, thread through rem sts to close ear.

EYE PATCH

Using circular needle and C, CO 6 sts and join for working in the rnd using Magic Loop method, making sure not to twist sts. PM to indicate beg of rnd.

Rnd 1: K1f&b all sts. (12 sts)

Rnd 2: (K1f&b, K1) around. (18 sts)

Rnd 3: (K1f&b, K2) around. (24 sts)

Rnd 4: (K1f&b, K3) around. (30 sts)

Rnd 5: (K1f&b, K4) around. (36 sts)

Rnds 6 and 7: Knit all sts.

Rnd 8: Loosely BO all sts.

SECOND-BIGGEST RING

Referring to directions for biggest ring on page 94 and "Making Stuffed Rings," make second-biggest ring with D.

CO 100 sts. Knit until piece measures 9" from CO edge. Close as for biggest ring.

ARM (MAKE 2.)

Using longer circular needle and D, CO 14 sts and join for working in the rnd using Magic Loop method, making sure not to twist sts. PM to indicate beg of rnd.

Rnds 1–30: Knit all sts.

Rnd 31: K1f&b all sts. (28 sts)

Rnds 32–43: Knit all sts.

Rnd 44: K2tog around. (14 sts)

Rnd 45: K2tog around. (7 sts)

Cut yarn and using tapestry needle, thread through rem sts to close hand.

FOOT (MAKE 2.)

Using longer circular needle and E, CO 18 sts and join for working in the rnd using Magic Loop method, making sure not to twist sts. PM to indicate beg of rnd.

Rnd 1: Knit all sts.

Rnd 2: (K1f&b, K7, K1f&b) twice. (22 sts)

Rnd 3: Knit all sts.

Rnd 4: (K1f&b, K9, K1f&b) twice. (26 sts)

Rnd 5: Knit all sts.

Rnd 6: (K1f&b, K11, K1f&b) twice. (30 sts)

Rnds 7–17: Knit all sts.

Rnd 18: (K4, K1f&b, K1f&b, K3, K1f&b, K1f&b, K4) twice. (38 sts)

Turn foot inside out, divide sts evenly on the 2 needle tips, and work 3-needle BO on all sts. Turn foot RS out.

EAR (MAKE 2.)

Using longer circular needle and E, CO 12 sts and join for working in the rnd using Magic Loop method, making sure not to twist sts. PM to indicate beg of rnd.

Rnd 1: Knit all sts.

Rnd 2: (K1f&b, K5) twice. (14 sts)

Rnd 3: Knit all sts.

Rnd 4: (K6, K1f&b) twice. (16 sts)

Rnds 5–20: Knit all sts.

Rnd 21: K2tog around. (8 sts)

Cut yarn and using tapestry needle, thread through rem sts to close ear.

MIDDLE RING

Referring to directions for biggest ring and "Making Stuffed Rings," make middle ring with E.

CO 90 sts. Knit until piece measures 8" from CO edge. Close as for biggest ring.

ARM (MAKE 2.)

Using longer circular needle and E, CO 18 sts and join for working in the rnd using Magic Loop method, making sure not to twist sts. PM to indicate beg of rnd.

Rnds 1–17: Knit all sts.

Rnd 18: K2tog around. (9 sts)

Cut yarn and using tapestry needle, thread through rem sts to close hand.

LEG (MAKE 2.)

Using longer circular needle and B, CO 20 sts and join for working in the rnd using Magic Loop method, making sure not to twist sts. PM to indicate beg of rnd.

Rnd 1: Knit all sts.

Rnd 2: (K1f&b, K8, K1f&b) twice. (24 sts)

Rnds 3–13: Knit all sts.

Rnd 14: K2tog around. (12 sts)

Cut yarn and using tapestry needle, thread through rem sts to close foot.

EAR (MAKE 2.)

Using longer circular needle and B, CO 12 sts and join for working in the rnd using Magic Loop method, making sure not to twist sts. PM to indicate beg of rnd.

Rnd 1: Knit all sts.

Rnd 2: (K1f&b, K4, K1f&b) twice. (16 sts)

Rnd 3: (K1f&b, K6, K1f&b) twice. (20 sts)

Rnds 4–12: Knit all sts.

Rnd 13: K2tog around. (10 sts)

Cut yarn and using tapestry needle, thread through rem sts to close ear.

SECOND-SMALLEST RING

Referring to directions for biggest ring and "Making Stuffed Rings," make second-smallest ring with F.

CO 80 sts. Knit until piece measures 7" from CO edge. Close as for biggest ring.

ARM (MAKE 2.)

Using longer circular needle and F, CO 16 sts and join for working in the rnd using Magic Loop method, making sure not to twist sts. PM to indicate beg of rnd.

Rnds 1–36: Knit all sts.

Rnd 37: K2tog around. (8 sts)

Cut yarn and using tapestry needle, thread through rem sts to close hand.

FOOT (MAKE 2.)

Using longer circular needle and A, CO 14 sts and join for working in the rnd using Magic Loop method, making sure not to twist sts. PM to indicate beg of rnd.

Rnd 1: Knit all sts.

Rnd 2: (K1f&b, K5, K1f&b) twice. (18 sts)

Rnd 3: Knit all sts.

Rnd 4: (K1f&b, K7, K1f&b) twice. (22 sts)

Rnd 5: Knit all sts.

Rnd 6: (K1f&b, K9, K1f&b) twice. (26 sts)

Rnds 7–16: Knit all sts.

Rnd 17: K2tog around. (13 sts)

Rnd 18: K2tog around, ending K1. (7 sts)

Cut yarn and using tapestry needle, thread through rem sts to close foot.

EAR (MAKE 2.)

Using longer circular needle and A, CO 14 sts and join for working in the rnd using Magic Loop method, making sure not to twist sts. PM to indicate beg of rnd.

Rnd 1: Knit all sts.

Rnd 2: (K1f&b, K6) twice. (16 sts)

Rnd 3: Knit all sts.

Rnd 4: (K7, K1f&b) twice. (18 sts)

Rnd 5: Knit all sts.

Rnd 6: (K1f&b, K8) twice. (20 sts)

Rnd 7: Knit all sts.

Rnd 8: (K9, K1f&b) twice. (22 sts)

Rnd 9: Knit all sts.

Rnd 10: (K1f&b, K10) twice. (24 sts)

Rnd 11: Knit all sts.

Rnd 12: (K11, K1f&b) twice. (26 sts)

Rnd 13: Knit all sts.

Rnd 14: (K1f&b, K12) twice. (28 sts)

Rnd 15: Knit all sts.

Rnd 16: (K13, K1f&b) twice. (30 sts)

Rnds 17 and 18: Knit all sts.

Divide sts evenly on the 2 needle tips and work 3-needle BO on all sts.

SMALLEST RING

Referring to directions for biggest ring and "Making Stuffed Rings," make smallest ring with C.

CO 70 sts. Knit until piece measures 6" from CO edge. Close as for biggest ring.

ARM (MAKE 2.)

Using longer circular needle and C, CO 12 sts and join for working in the rnd using Magic Loop method, making sure not to twist sts. PM to indicate beg of rnd.

Rnds 1–24: Knit all sts.

Rnd 25: K2tog around. (6 sts)

Cut yarn and using tapestry needle, thread through rem sts to close hand.

FOOT (MAKE 2.)

Using longer circular needle and E, CO 12 sts and join for working in the rnd using Magic Loop method, making sure not to twist sts. PM to indicate beg of rnd.

Rnds 1–3: Knit all sts.

Rnd 4: (K1f&b, K5) twice. (14 sts)

Rnd 5: Knit all sts.

Rnd 6: (K6, K1f&b) twice. (16 sts)

Rnd 7: Knit all sts.

Rnd 8: (K1f&b, K7) twice. (18 sts)

Rnd 9: Knit all sts.

Rnd 10: (K8, K1f&b) twice. (20 sts)

Rnds 11–15: Knit all sts.

Turn foot inside out, divide sts evenly on the 2 needle tips, and work 3-needle BO on all sts. Turn foot RS out.

EAR (MAKE 2.)

Using either needle and E, CO 5 sts. *Do not join.*

Rnd 1: Purl all sts.

Rnd 2: K1f&b, K3, K1f&b. (7 sts)

Rnd 3: Purl all sts.

Rnd 4: K1f&b, K5, K1f&b. (9 sts)

Rnds 5–11: Work in St st.

Rnd 12: Ssk, K5, K2tog. (7 sts)

Rnd 13: Purl all sts.

Rnd 14: Ssk, K3, K2tog. (5 sts)

Rnd 15: Purl all sts.

Rnd 16: Ssk, K1, K2tog. (3 sts)

Rnd 17: P3tog.

Cut yarn and using a tapestry needle, pull through last st.

BASE

Using 40" circular needle and A, CO 4 sts and join for working in the rnd using Magic Loop method, making sure not to twist sts. PM to indicate beg of rnd.

Rnd 1: K1f&b all sts. (8 sts)

Rnd 2: K1f&b all sts. (16 sts)

Rnd 3: (K2, PM) around. You'll have 8 markers on needle.

Rnd 4: (K1f&b, knit to marker, sl marker) around. (24 sts)

Rnd 5: Knit all sts.

Rep rnds 4 and 5 until you have 200 sts (25 sts between each set of markers). As project gets bigger, and won't fit on Magic Loop any longer, transfer sts to 24" circular needle.

Loosely BO all sts.

Using 40" needle and A, PU 200 sts from bound-off edge. Knit all sts until piece measures 4" from PU edge.

Next rnd: Purl all sts to make turning ridge, and PM every 25 sts. You'll have 8 markers total.

Rnd 1: (K2tog, K23, PM) around.

Rnd 2: Knit all sts.

Rnd 3: (K2tog, knit to marker, sl marker) around.

Rep rnds 2 and 3 until 32 sts rem, moving sts to 40" circular needle and using Magic Loop when there are too few sts to knit on the 24" circular. Stuff base, working with round shape and pushing stuffing to outside edge to create circle, then filling in center. I understuffed this part since I wanted it flat for the stackers to sit on.

Work last 32 sts in the rnd to form a pole. Stuffing as you go, knit until pole measures 13" from last dec rnd. Be sure to stuff this part quite firmly so it will stand on its own. (You might choose to add a chopstick to the base of the pole to keep it standing up straight, but do think of baby safety before doing so.)

Next rnd: (K2tog, K2) around. (24 sts)

Knit 1 rnd.

Next rnd: (K2tog, K1) around. (16 sts)

Knit 1 rnd.

Next rnd: (K2tog) around. (8 sts)

Add any last bits of stuffing. Cut yarn and using tapestry needle, thread through rem sts to close pole.

FINISHING

Weave in all ends. Refer to "Monster-Making University" (page 15) for detailed monster-finishing directions. Stuff all limbs and refer to photos to make your monsters. Embroider eyes and toss your "O" monsters onto the stacker.

Set the stacker on the floor and get ready for hours of baby entertainment!

Monster
BLOCKS

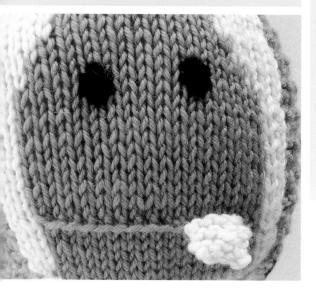

Here's yet another monsterized take on an old classic. I love soft blocks, and every baby I have ever known loves them too. They're great for stacking and tossing around, and soft enough to go in curious baby mouths. What could be better?!

Skill Level: Intermediate

Finished Size: Approx 4" x 4" x 4" stuffed

MATERIALS (TO MAKE ALL 5 BLOCKS)

A 1 skein of 220 Superwash from Cascade Yarns (100% superwash wool; 100 g/3.5 oz; 220 yds/200 m) in color 817 Aran

B 1 skein of 220 Superwash from Cascade Yarns in color 886 Citron

C 1 skein of 220 Superwash from Cascade Yarns in color 810 Teal

D 1 skein of 220 Superwash from Cascade Yarns in color 1973 Seafoam Heather

E 1 skein of 220 Superwash from Cascade Yarns in color 815 Black

Set of U.S. size 5 (3.75 mm) needles, or size needed to obtain gauge

Scrap of white yarn for teeth

Scrap of black yarn for embroidering eyes

Notions: Stuffing, row counter (optional), tapestry needle

GAUGE

22 sts and 28 rows = 4" in St st

BLOCK (MAKE 5.)

Each block has 6 sides. Start with the monster face, then pick up sts and continue with the next side until all 6 sides have been worked.

MONSTER-FACE SIDE

CO 22 sts in A.

Work rows 1–28 of monster-face chart on page 103.

Loosely BO all sts.

Tooth: With top of head facing upside down, count from left edge (when looking at piece upside down) to 6th st of mouth line. Beg in 6th st, PU 4 sts in 6th through 3rd sts.

Using A, knit 5 rows (garter st).

BO all sts.

BLUE-STRIPES SIDE

Using C, with RS facing you PU 22 sts from bound-off edge of monster-face side. This counts as row 1 of the stripe patt.

Work in St st, alternating 4 rows C and 4 rows D until you have 7 total stripes (you'll end with a C stripe).

Loosely BO all sts.

POLKA-DOT SIDE

Using E, with RS facing you PU 22 sts from bound-off edge of blue-stripes side. This counts as row 1 of chart.

Knit rows 2–28 of polka-dot chart (right).

Loosely BO all sts.

BLACK-AND-WHITE-STRIPES SIDE

Using A, with RS facing you PU 22 sts from bound-off edge of polka-dot side. This counts as row 1 of the stripe patt.

Work in St st, alternating 4 rows A and 2 rows E until you have 9 stripes (you'll end with 4 rows of A stripe).

Loosely BO all sts.

GREEN TEXTURED-STITCH SIDE

Using B, with RS facing you PU 23 sts from right-hand side of blue-stripes side.

Row 1: Knit all sts. (For the first rep this is the PU row.)

Row 2: Knit all sts.

Row 3: K1, *sl 1 wyib, K1; rep from *.

Row 4: K1, *sl 1 wyif, K1; rep from *.

Rows 5 and 6: Knit all sts.

Row 7: K2, *sl 1 wyib, K1; rep from * to last st, K1.

Row 8: K2, *sl 1 wyif, K1; rep from * to last st, K1.

Rep rows 1–8 until side measures 4".

Loosely BO all sts.

RIPPLE-STITCH SIDE

Using D, PU 22 sts from left-hand side of blue-stripes side.

Purl 1 row.

Row 1: K6, *P2, K6; rep from *.

Row 2: K1, *P4, K4; rep from * to last 5 sts, P4, K1.

Row 3: P2, *K2, P2; rep from *.

Row 4: P1, *K4, P4; rep from * to last 5 sts, K4, P1.

Row 5: K2, *P2, K6; rep from * to last 4 sts, P2, K2.

Row 6: P6, *K2, P6; rep from *.

Row 7: P1, *P2, K2; rep from * to last 5 sts, K4, P1.

Row 8: K2, *P2, K2; rep from *.

Row 9: K1, *P4, K4; rep from * to last 5 sts, P4, K1.

Row 10: P2, *K2, P6; rep from * to last 4 sts, K2, P2.

Rep rows 1–10 until side measures 4".

Loosely BO all sts.

FINISHING

Weave in all ends. Block as desired. Use st-to-st mattress st (page 32) to sew CO edge of monster-face side to bound-off edge of black-and-white-stripes side. Sew the 2 sides into ring to create cube, using row-to-row mattress st (page 35) on sides where sts run parallel to each other, and ladder st on sides where sts run in different directions.

Stuff cube, aiming for as square a shape as you can get. It's helpful to push stuffing into each corner to get your cube to look more square. If you prefer, you can buy foam squares that measure 4" to get a more square block. Once you've stuffed your blocks, sew up the last side.

Go find a baby to play with your new toys!

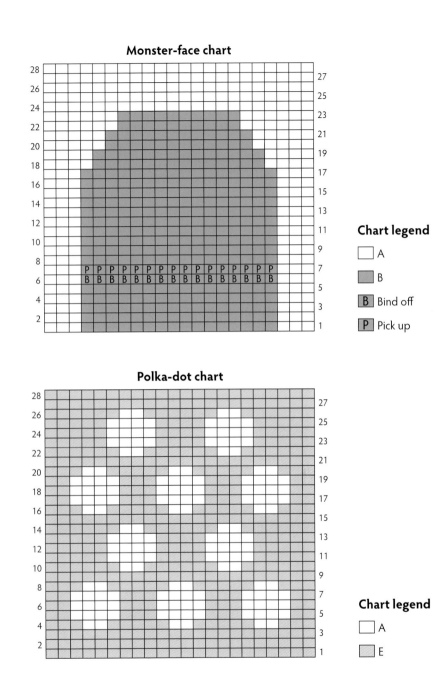

Monster-face chart

Chart legend

☐ A

▨ B

Ⓑ Bind off

Ⓟ Pick up

Polka-dot chart

Chart legend

☐ A

▨ E

Monster RATTLES

My feeling is, no baby toy box is complete without a rattle or two. Presley's feeling on toys is, the noisier the better! Monster rattles are the perfect complement to these feelings. I designed these to be easy for little hands to grab, and knitted in a fluffy cotton, they're soft for baby fingers (and in baby mouths).

Skill Level: Intermediate

Finished Size:

- Roundy Rattle: 6" tall
- Circle Rattle: 13" head to toe

MATERIALS

For Green-and-White Circle Rattle

A 1 skein of Comfy Fingering from Knit Picks (75% pima cotton, 25% acrylic; 50 g; 218 yds) in color Pea Pod [1]

B 1 skein of Comfy Fingering from Knit Picks in color White

For Blue-Stripe Roundy Rattle

C 1 skein of Comfy Fingering from Knit Picks in color Marlin

D 1 skein of Comfy Fingering from Knit Picks in color Sea Foam

For Both Rattles

U.S. size 1 (2.25 mm) 40" circular needle (for Magic Loop method), or size needed to obtain gauge

1 additional circular needle, any length, in same size as 40" circular needle (for 3-needle BO and holding provisional CO sts)

Scrap of black yarn for face

Notions: Stuffing, rattle insert, row counter (optional), stitch marker, tapestry needle, straight pins (to help with assembly)

GAUGE

32 sts and 44 rows = 4" in St st

CIRCLE RATTLE

With 40" circular needle, waste yarn, and A, use provisional CO to CO 70 sts. *Do not join.*

Knit 1 row. Divide sts in half on each needle tip to work in the round using Magic Loop method (page 7). Join, working from last st knitted to first st knitted.

Knit until piece measures 3" from CO edge.

Referring to "Making Stuffed Rings" on page 11, move provisional CO sts from waste yarn to additional circular needle. Pull this needle up through center of ring you've just knit (make sure RS is outside) and use tapestry needle to work Kitchener st to close ring, stopping to stuff ring every couple inches. The provisional CO makes every other st twisted on the waste yarn, so be sure to untwist sts as you go by knitting into the back of these twisted sts. When you've worked all sts and ring is completely stuffed, close up any hole that is left. If you end up one st short, PU extra st at end.

HEAD

Using 40" circular needle and B, CO 52 sts and join for working in the rnd using Magic Loop method, making sure not to twist sts. PM to indicate beg of rnd.

Circle rattle

Rnds 1–15: Knit all sts, alternating 3 rnds B and 3 rnds A.

Rnd 16: With A, (ssk, K22, K2tog) twice. (48 sts)

Rnd 17: (Ssk, K20, K2tog) twice. (44 sts)

Rnd 18: (Ssk, K18, K2tog) twice. (40 sts)

Rnd 19: (Ssk, K16, K2tog) twice. (36 sts)

Turn head inside out, divide sts evenly on the 2 needle tips, and work 3-needle BO on all sts. Turn head RS out.

ARM (MAKE 2.)

Using 40" circular needle and B, CO 16 sts and join for working in the rnd using Magic Loop method, making sure not to twist sts. PM to indicate beg of rnd.

Rnds 1–57: Knit all sts, alternating 3 rnds B and 3 rnds A, ending with 3 rnds B.

Rnd 58: With B, K2tog around. (8 sts)

Stuff arm. Cut yarn and using tapestry needle, thread through rem sts to close hand.

LEG (MAKE 2.)

Using 40" circular needle and B, CO 18 sts and join for working in the rnd using Magic Loop method, making sure not to twist sts. PM to indicate beg of rnd.

Rnds 1–42: Knit all sts, alternating 3 rnds B and 3 rnds A.

Rnd 43: Cont in established stripe patt, K7, K1f&b in next 4 sts, K7. (22 sts)

Rnd 44: K9, K1f&b in next 4 sts, K9. (26 sts)

Rnd 45: K11, K1f&b in next 4 sts, K11. (30 sts)

Rnd 46: K13, K1f&b in next 4 sts, K13. (34 sts)

Rnd 47: K16, K1f&b in next 2 sts, K16. (36 sts)

Rnds 48–56: Knit all sts in established stripe patt.

Rnd 57: With B, (ssk, K14, K2tog) twice. (32 sts)

Stuff foot. Cut yarn, leaving long tail, and use tapestry needle to work Kitchener st to close foot.

EAR (MAKE 2.)

Using 40" circular needle and B, CO 8 sts and join for working in the rnd using Magic Loop method, making sure not to twist sts. PM to indicate beg of rnd.

The ear is worked in stripes, alternating 3 rnds B and 3 rnds A.

Rnd 1: Knit all sts.

Rnd 2: (K1f&b, K3) twice. (10 sts)

Rnd 3: (K4, K1f&b) twice. (12 sts)

Rnds 4–10: Knit all sts.

Rnd 11: (Ssk, K2, K2tog) twice. (8 sts)

Rnd 12: Knit all sts.

Cut yarn and using tapestry needle, thread through rem sts to close ear.

ROUNDY RATTLE

Using 40" circular needle and C, CO 6 sts and join for working in the rnd using Magic Loop method, making sure not to twist sts. PM to indicate beg of rnd.

The body is worked in stripes, alternating 5 rnds C and 5 rnds D.

Rnd 1: K1f&b all sts. (12 sts)

Rnd 2: K1f&b all sts. (24 sts)

Rnd 3: Knit all sts.

Rnd 4: (K1f&b, K1) around. (36 sts)

Rnd 5: Knit all sts.

Rnd 6: (K1f&b, K2) around. (48 sts)

Rnd 7: Knit all sts.

Rnd 8: (K1f&b, K3) around. (60 sts)

Rnds 9–30: Knit all sts.

Rnd 31: (Ssk, K26, K2tog) twice. (56 sts)

Rnd 32: Knit all sts.

Rnd 33: (Ssk, K24, K2tog) twice. (52 sts)

Rnd 34: Knit all sts.

Rnd 35: (Ssk, K22, K2tog) twice. (48 sts)

Rnd 36: Knit all sts.

Rnd 37: (Ssk, K20, K2tog) twice. (44 sts)

Rnd 38: Knit all sts.

Rnd 39: (Ssk, K18, K2tog) twice. (40 sts)

Rnd 40: (K2tog, K3) around. (32 sts)

Rnds 41–62: Switch to C and cont to end, knit all sts.

Rnd 63: (Ssk, K12, K2tog) twice. (28 sts)

Rnd 64: (Ssk, K10, K2tog) twice. (24 sts)

Rnd 65: (Ssk, K8, K2tog) twice. (20 sts)

Rnd 66: (Ssk, K16, K2tog) twice. (16 sts)

Stuff body now, being sure to add rattle insert. Cut yarn, leaving long tail, and use tapestry needle to work Kitchener st to close head.

ARM (MAKE 2.)

Using 40" circular needle and C, CO 12 sts and join for working in the rnd using Magic Loop method, making sure not to twist sts. PM to indicate beg of rnd.

Rnds 1–30: Knit all sts.

Rnd 31: Switch to D and knit all sts. Cont with D to end.

Rnd 32: (K1f&b, K1) around. (18 sts)

Roundy rattle

Rnds 33–44: Knit all sts.

Rnd 45: K2tog around. (9 sts)

Stuff the hand now. Cut yarn and using tapestry needle, thread through rem sts to close hand.

EAR (MAKE 2.)

Using either circular needle, CO 4 sts in D. *Do not join.*

Row 1: Purl all sts.

Row 2: K1f&b, K2, K1f&b. (6 sts)

Row 3: Purl all sts.

Row 4: K1f&b, K4, K1f&b. (8 sts)

Rows 5–9: Work in St st.

Row 10: Ssk, K4, K2tog. (6 sts)

Row 11: P2tog 3 times. (3 sts)

Row 12: K3tog.

Cut yarn and using tapestry needle, thread through rem st to close ear.

FINISHING

Weave in all ends. Referring to "Monster-Making University" on page 15, start assembling your rattles by placing arms on sides of Roundy Rattle in top D stripe. Whipstitch half of head onto ring, stuff head, add rattle insert, and then finish stitching down head. Using head as a guide, whipstitch arms and legs onto ring to finish rattle.

Hand the rattles to a kiddo and let the noisemaking begin!

Abbreviations/Glossary

( ) Work instructions within parentheses as many times as directed

approx approximately

beg begin(ning)

BO bind off

CC contrasting color

CO cast on

cont continue(ing)(s)

dec(s) decrease(ing)(s)

dpn(s) double-pointed needle(s)

g gram(s)

inc increase(ing)(s)

join begin to knit in the round

K knit

K1f&b knit into front and back of same stitch— 1 stitch increased

K2tog knit 2 stitches together—1 stitch decreased

m meter(s)

MC main color

mm millimeter(s)

oz ounce(s)

P purl

P1f&b purl into front and back of same stitch— 1 stitch increased

P2tog purl 2 stitches together—1 stitch decreased

patt(s) pattern(s)

PM place marker

PU pick up and knit

pw purlwise

rem remain(ing)(s)

rep(s) repeat(s)

rnd(s) round(s)

RS right side

sl slip

sl 1 slip 1 stitch purlwise unless otherwise indicated

sl 1-P1-psso slip 1 stitch, purl 1 stitch, pass slipped stitch over purl stitch— 1 stitch decreased

ssk slip 2 stitches knitwise, 1 at a time, to right needle, then insert left needle from left to right into front loops and knit 2 stitches together—1 stitch decreased

st(s) stitch(es)

St st(s) stockinette stitch(es)

tbl through back loop(s)

tog together

WS wrong side

wyib with yarn in back

wyif with yarn in front

yd(s) yard(s)

Where to Get the Goods

Contact the following yarn companies to find shops in your area that carry the yarns featured in this book.

Berroco
www.berroco.com
Comfort, Comfort DK, Vintage, Vintage Chunky

Cascade Yarns
www.cascadeyarns.com
Heritage, 220 Superwash

HiKoo
www.skacelknitting.com
Simplicity, SimpliWorsted

Knit Picks
www.knitpicks.com
Comfy Fingering, Comfy Worsted, Stroll Multi Sock, Swish DK

Lorna's Laces
www.lornaslaces.net
Shepherd Bulky, Shepherd Sock, Shepherd Sport, Shepherd Worsted

Shibuiknits
www.shibuiknits.com
Merino Worsted, Shibui Sock

Spud & Chloë
www.spudandchloe.com
Fine, Sweater

Safety eyes, buttons, pillow forms, and embroidery hoops can be found at most major craft stores, or many places online. I carry safety eyes in all the sizes shown in this book on my website: www.dangercrafts.com.

Body-pillow inserts can be purchased at Target.

Inexpensive comforters can be purchased at Ikea.

Fishing-line swivel and monofilament for mobile can be found where fishing supplies are sold.

Rattle inserts can be found many places online. I found mine on etsy.com by searching for "Rattle Inserts."

Standard Yarn-Weight System

Yarn-Weight Symbol and Category Name	**1** Super Fine	**2** Fine	**3** Light	**4** Medium	**5** Bulky	**6** Super Bulky
Types of Yarn in Category	Sock, Fingering, Baby	Sport, Baby	DK, Light Worsted	Worsted, Afghan, Aran	Chunky, Craft, Rug	Bulky, Roving
Knit Gauge Range* in Stockinette Stitch to 4"	27 to 32 sts	23 to 26 sts	21 to 24 sts	16 to 20 sts	12 to 15 sts	6 to 11 sts
Recommended Needle in Metric Size Range	2.25 to 3.25 mm	3.25 to 3.75 mm	3.75 to 4.5 mm	4.5 to 5.5 mm	5.5 to 8 mm	8 mm and larger
Recommended Needle in U.S. Size Range	1 to 3	3 to 5	5 to 7	7 to 9	9 to 11	11 and larger

These are guidelines only. The above reflect the most commonly used gauges and needle sizes for specific yarn categories.

Acknowledgments

First off, just an all-around big thank-you to everyone for making this book possible. I love writing, and it's such a big thrill that I'm able to write my second book. I'd like to extend a special thank-you to the following:

* To the folks at Martingale, for believing in yet another of my wacky ideas.

* To my agent, Linda, for talking me through, encouraging me, answering my questions, and being all-around awesome.

* To Mr. Danger, I know I was a challenge through this! Thank you for all the monster-face embroidery, monster naming (even if all you could think of was "Jimmy"), support and encouragement, and for putting up with me in general. You're amazing and my favorite human.

* To Presley, for being the amazing kiddo that you are, the inspiration, and the product tester.

* To my family for the continued support and encouragement.

* To Aja and Susan, two knitting superstars. Thanks for the knitting help—you kept me out of the looney bin! At least for now.

* To all of the yarn companies for so generously donating the yarn in this book.

* And to my fabulous customers—for continuing to support my monster-mania!